Mrs. Lahti

EGGS
THE FINE ART OF EGG, OMELET AND SOUFFLÉ COOKING

PUBLISHER: R. ARTHUR BARRETT
EDITOR: CAROL D. BRENT
ART DIRECTOR: DICK COLLINS
PHOTOGRAPHY BY BILL MILLER

Book Trade Distribution by
DOUBLEDAY & COMPANY, INC.
Garden City, New York

TESTED RECIPE PUBLISHERS, INC. CHICAGO

CONTENTS

FIRST EDITION/FIRST PRINTING

Library of Congress Catalog Card Number 73-122450

OTHER *Gourmet* INTERNATIONAL™ BOOKS:

BLENDING: The Fine Art of Modern Blending
FONDUE: The Fine Art of Fondue, Chinese Wok and Chafing Dish Cooking
PANCAKES & WAFFLES: The Fine Art of Pancake, Waffle, Crêpe and Blintz Cooking

FROM **trp**™ AND DOUBLEDAY OF COURSE...

INTRODUCTION

Wonderful Wonderful Eggs...Eggs have been considered very special foods since ancient times. No food is quite as essential for good cooking and eating as the ordinary egg, valued too because it's so handy, always in season, inexpensive, versatile, easy and quick to fix and nutritious.

Eggs are truly the cooks best friend whether they are fried or transformed into handsome aristocratic soufflés, feather-light omelets, satin smooth custards or popovers puffed to fantastic size. Eggs do so much, so much better; they thicken sauces and puddings, give lightness to cakes, emulsify mayonnaise and salad dressings, make crystal free ice creams, icings and candies, hold the lowly meat loaf together and add a decorative touch to appetizers, casseroles, salads and cold meat trays.

No doubt the egg is one of nature's most perfect foods...fine for the hale and hearty or the invalid and a bargain for dieters, too. Only 77 to 80 calories in a two-ounce egg. Two eggs furnish 17% of the daily adult protein requirement, amino acids for building body tissues and vitally important vitamins A, D, E, K, B_6, B_{12}, thiamin, riboflavin and niacin.

Don't take eggs for granted...look over the following pages. Included are money saving buying tips, ways to store and use eggs and recipes by the dozens for everyday and elegant foods to serve from breakfast through late evening suppers.

To help you select recipes which are different and have a foreign flair we have placed this seal next to the recipe title *Gourmet* INTERNATIONAL

EGG HOW TO'S

Eggs Are Always In Season!

Gone are the days when fresh eggs were plentiful each spring and had to be preserved for use during the winter months. Today's egg production is a streamlined round-the-clock business geared to keep a steady supply of fine fresh eggs coming to market the year around.

Egg Buying Tips

Egg Grades—Know the egg grades. Eggs are graded for freshness and quality, select ones packed in cartons which give both grade and size of eggs.

Prices vary for eggs of different sizes but of the same grade. Use the following grade and size charts to get the best egg buys.

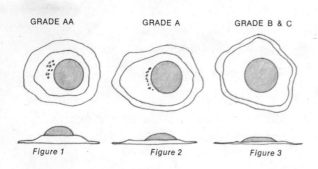

GRADE AA   GRADE A   GRADE B & C

Figure 1   Figure 2   Figure 3

Grade	Comment
AA	Fancy fresh, top quality. The yolk is centered and well rounded and white is firm. (Fig. 1). These eggs have the best appearance. Most desirable for poaching, frying and baking.
A	Fine fresh, quality eggs. Excellent for table use, cooking or baking (Fig. 2).
B & C	Less expensive, less attractive. Excellent for making scrambled eggs, omelets or for cooking and baking (Fig 3).

Egg Sizes—Eggs are available in the following sizes although large, medium and small eggs are in greatest supply.

Size	12 eggs must weight at least
Jumbo	30 oz. or 1 lb. 14 oz.
Extra Large	27 oz. or 1 lb. 11 oz.
Large	24 oz. or 1 lb. 8 oz.
Medium	21 oz. or 1 lb. 5 oz.
Small	18 oz. or 1 lb. 2 oz.

Pick Right Size Eggs—Recipes calling for eggs, as a rule, have been tested with **large** or **medium** size eggs (24 to 21 oz. per dozen). Never use extra large or jumbo eggs for cooking or baking unless the recipe specifically calls for them.

Small eggs (18 oz. per dozen) are ideal for serving children, convalescents and weight watchers.

Jumbo or extra large eggs are very large and one egg rather than two is usually considered a serving.

Color of Shell—The color of the egg shell is determined by the diet and the breed of hen. There's no difference in the quality, cooking, food value or flavor of eggs with brown, white or speckled shells. Eggs with white shells are preferred in most areas of the U.S.A., brown or speckled ones in some areas. Very often eggs with shells of the preferred color in an area are more expensive. Nut brown eggs are the rage in England and on the Continent. Gastronomes all over Europe pay a premium for large brown eggs.

Eggs Must Be Kept Cold!—Buy eggs in cartons from a dealer who keeps them refrigerated, they will be fresher when purchased and keep longer. Transfer eggs to home refrigerator as soon as possible.

To Separate Eggs

Separate one well chilled egg at a time and transfer yolks and whites to separate bowls. To separate each egg crack shell at the center of egg by giving it a sharp tap on edge of a custard cup (Fig. 4).

Hold egg over cup; pull shell halves apart holding egg yolk in ½ of shell, letting egg white run into cup (Fig. 5).

Transfer egg yolk carefully from one half of shell to the other until all egg white has drained off (Fig. 6). Empty yolk still in ½ of shell, into a separate cup or bowl (Fig. 7). Repeat as necessary.

Should any bit of yolk get into whites remove it with tip of spoon or corner of paper towel. Even a small amount of yolk in egg white will keep it from beating.

Figure 4   Figure 5

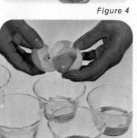

Figure 6   Figure 7

To Store Eggs

Eggs must be kept cold! Buy them from a refrigerated case and put them in the home refrigerator as soon as possible. Plan to use eggs within 7 to 10 days.

Egg shells are porous so store eggs, large end up, in carton or egg compartment of refrigerator away from strong flavored foods.

Never wash eggs until ready to use them. Washing will remove a protective film from shell that helps to keep eggs fresh.

Left Over Egg Yolks—Turn them into a small jar; cover with a film of cold water; cover tightly. Refrigerate 1 or 2 days.

Left Over Egg Whites—Pour into small jar; cover tightly. Refrigerate 1 or 2 days.

To Freeze Eggs

Whole Raw Eggs Or Egg Yolks—Pour eggs into small moisture proof freezer jar or container. Add ½ teaspoon salt or 3 teaspoons sugar to each ½ cup of raw whole eggs or egg yolks; mix. Seal container; label, date and freeze.

Egg Whites—Same as for whole eggs (above) except omit salt or sugar.

Frozen Egg Equivalents

Substitute:
   3 tablespoons frozen whole eggs for 1 whole egg
   1 to 1½ tablespoons frozen egg yolks for 1 egg yolk
   2 tablespoons frozen egg whites for 1 egg white.

Guide for Measuring Eggs

Use the following chart as a guide if recipes call for a cup measure of eggs.

For 1 cup (8 oz.) of eggs use

Size	Whole Eggs	Egg Whites	Egg Yolks
Large	5	7-8	12-14
Medium	6	8-9	14-16
Small	7	9-10	15-19

To Beat Eggs

Whole eggs, whites and yolks beat to the greatest volume if allowed to warm to room temperature before beating.

Egg Whites—Use a clean dry bowl with rounded bottom, large enough to allow egg whites to increase in volume 4 times. Some chefs insist upon a copper bowl claiming there is a chemical reaction between the egg whites and the copper. This fact has not been substantiated. Use a wire whisk, rotary beater, or hand or electric mixer for beating egg whites. Never use a blender to beat egg whites!

Egg whites beat to a greater volume, are stiffer and more stable when a small amount of acid such as cream of tartar, lemon juice or vinegar is added. Use ⅛ teaspoon cream of tartar or ½ teaspoon vinegar or lemon juice for each 3 egg whites used. Add acid to whites after beating egg whites to the foamy stage.

"Beat egg whites slightly or until foamy."—Egg whites are beaten until frothy, have large air bubbles and will pour or flow easily (Fig. 1).

"Beat egg whites until they form soft peaks."—Air cells will be tiny, eggs white, surface glossy and have a moist appearance and whites will hold a soft peak which tends to curve over. Beaten whites will slip slightly when bowl is tipped (Fig. 2).

"Beat egg whites until they form stiff peaks, but not dry."—Same as for "soft peaks" (above) except peaks stand up straight rather than curve over (Fig. 3).

"Beat egg yolks until thick and lemon colored"—Use a small bowl; beat with rotary beater or electric mixer until air bubbles are small, mixture is very thick and a very light yellow color.

WISK   ELECTRIC MIXER

Figure 1

Figure 2

Figure 3

COOKING EGGS

Baking...Easiest Way to Cook Eggs!

Bake eggs when serving eggs to a crowd for breakfast or brunch . . . it's wonderfully easy. Just fill the baking dishes ahead of time, cover and refrigerate until 10 minutes before cooking time. Let stand at room temperature while oven is heating and bake them while the bacon frizzles and coffee brews.

Brush small 1 or 2-egg ramekins (Fig. 1) or shirred egg dishes with melted butter or margarine. Break 1 or 2 eggs into each dish; add a tablespoonful of light cream and season with salt and pepper. Place on tray; bake in slow oven (325°F.) 15 to 20 minutes or until eggs are the firmness desired. Serve in baking dishes.

Shirred Eggs, French Style

Fanciers of shirred eggs should have small individual flameproof 2-egg china, aluminum, copper (Fig. 2) or iron frying pans for preparing Shirred Eggs, French Style. Melt 1 tablespoon butter or margarine in each pan, add 1 or 2 eggs to each pan and cook over very low heat until egg whites start to set on bottom of pan. Season with salt and pepper and transfer pans to moderate oven (350°F.) and finish baking eggs, 5 to 8 minutes or until whites are milky but soft.

Figure 1   Figure 2

Eggs en Cocotte

Prepare as directed for Baked Eggs (above) except for following changes: Bake each egg in a small well buttered ramekin or custard cup set in a pan filled with boiling water to within ½ inch of top of ramekins. Bake in moderate oven (350°F.) 10 to 15 minutes or until eggs are firmness desired.

Fried Eggs

Perfectly fried eggs are one of the world's finest foods, and certainly the favorite dish of most Americans. There are three basic types of fried eggs, the American (Fried Eggs à la Robert), basted and French fried ones. American style eggs and basted eggs are raw shelled eggs pan fried in a small amount of fat sunny-side-up, turned or basted until yolk is coated with a thin film of egg white. French or deep fat fried eggs are a bit unique but deliciously different.

Fried Eggs à la Robert

Melt or warm 2 tablespoons butter or margarine, bacon drippings or cooking oil in a 7-inch frying pan; heat gently. Break each egg into a cup or saucer. Slip 2 or 3 eggs into pan. Turn heat low, cover and cook 3 to 4 minutes or until yolk is cooked to desired doneness (Fig. 3). For firm egg yolks baste with hot fat during frying (Fig. 4) or turn and cook on both sides.

Figure 3   Figure 4

Basted Eggs

Prepare as directed for Fried Eggs à la Robert (this page) except uncover pan and add 1 teaspoon of water (for each egg being cooked) halfway through cooking process. Cover tightly and finish cooking. Basted eggs should not be turned during cooking.

Deep-Fat Fried Eggs

Heat cooking oil, about 1½ inches deep, in small saucepan to 385°F. Break eggs into saucer or cup. With one hand slide egg into hot oil, swirling oil carefully with wooden spoon with other hand. Cook about 30 seconds or until egg looks like a fritter (Fig. 5). Lift egg out with slotted spoon; drain on paper toweling. Serve with tomato, rarebit or other favorite entrée sauce.

French-Fried Eggs

Dip shelled hard-cooked or poached eggs into beaten eggs, then roll in fine bread or cereal crumbs. Chill 2 hours. Heat cooking oil, 1½ inches deep, in small saucepan to 385°F. Lower eggs, 1 or 2 at a time into hot oil and fry until golden brown (Fig. 6). Two halves of deviled eggs put together, coated and fried as directed above make delicious hors d'oeuvres.

Figure 5   Figure 6

Poached Eggs

Poached eggs are shelled raw eggs cooked in gently simmering water or steam. A well poached egg has the yolk pocketed in a thin film of egg white. Here are the favorite methods for poaching eggs.

Poached Eggs . . . American Style—Brush bottom of frying pan or shallow saucepan with butter or margarine. Add water to pan as needed to fill to a 2-inch depth. Add ½ teaspoon salt to water to improve flavor of egg white. Vinegar is not needed to firm egg white since it sets up at 140°F. Bring water to a gentle boil to center of pan. Lower heat so water simmers gently. Break egg into a saucer; hold edge of saucer just above water level and carefully slip egg into water. A lightly greased muffin or egg ring can be placed in the water so egg slipped into ring poaches with a uniform shape (Fig. 1). Keep water just below simmering point until egg white is set and yolk is cooked to doneness desired, 3 to 5 minutes. To remove egg from pan slip a slotted spoon or pancake turner under egg and lift above pan; drain and transfer to serving dish. If ring is used remove before removing egg from pan. If desired, eggs may be poached in milk, bouillon, meat or vegetable stock or sauces.

Figure 1   Figure 2

Cooking Eggs in a Poacher—There are scores of easy to use egg poachers available for poaching 1 to 6 eggs. Some are electric (Fig. 2), many are shaped to give cooked eggs an attractive shape. Follow cooking Instructions supplied by manufacturer of equipment.

Poached Eggs . . . French Style—Cook eggs, one at a time, in a small deep saucepan in 2½ to 3 inches of water. Add 1 tablespoon vinegar or lemon juice and 1 teaspoon salt to water for flavor. Hold egg in custard cup above water with one hand and stir boiling water, round and round, with other hand (Fig. 3), until a whirlpool forms in center of pan. Carefully slip egg into center of whirlpool and turn heat to low. Continue stirring carefully so egg will spin and form a slightly oval shaped poached egg (Fig. 4). If a thin tail of egg white forms trim it off before serving.

Figure 3   Figure 4

Scrambled Eggs

Scrambled eggs are raw shelled eggs which are whipped slightly, cooked in hot butter, margarine, oil or bacon fat over low heat, until done, stirring often. Chopped cooked meat, poultry or vegetables may be added to eggs before cooking for a delightfully different flavor.

Figure 5   Figure 6

Scrambled Eggs For Four—Melt 3 tablespoons butter or margarine in heavy skillet or electric frypan using moderate heat. Combine 8 eggs, ½ cup light cream or milk, ½ teaspoon salt and a dash of black pepper; beat slightly. Pour egg mixture into heated pan and cook to desired doneness, stirring often (Fig. 5). Serve at once. Yield: 4 servings.

Scrambled Eggs For Two—Cut recipe for Scrambled Eggs For Four (this page) in half.

Cheesy Scrambled Eggs—Sprinkle ¾ to 1 cup shredded pasteurized process American or Cheddar cheese over Scrambled Eggs For Four (this page) when set but still soft; mix gently. Serve on toast or waffle squares. Yield: 4 servings.

Chicken Livers and Eggs—Fold ½ cup crisp cooked crumbled bacon, 8 cooked chicken livers, cut in quarters, and 3 tablespoons catsup into Scrambled Eggs For Four (this page) just before they set. Yield: 4 servings.

Sausage Eggs—Cut 6 cooked pork sausage links crosswise into ½-inch slices. Fold sausage into Scrambled Eggs For Four (this page) just before they set. Yield: 4 servings.

Bacon or Ham Scrambled Eggs—Follow recipe for Scrambled Eggs For Four (this page) and stir ½ to ¾ cup crisp cooked crumbled bacon or finely chopped fully-cooked ham into egg mixture before cooking (Fig. 6). Yield: 4 servings.

Soft-Cooked Eggs I (Boiled)

Place eggs in saucepan. Cover eggs generously with cold water. Bring water to a boil quickly, remove from heat. Let eggs stand in water 3 to 6 minutes as desired (Fig. 1). Cool in cold water 1 or 2 minutes for easier handling.

Soft-Cooked Eggs II (Boiled)

Let eggs stand in pan of warm water 2 or 3 minutes. Carefully lower eggs with a spoon, 1 at a time, into a pan of rapidly boiling water deep enough to cover eggs. Simmer until desired firmness, 3 to 6 minutes. Cool in cold water 1 or 2 minutes for easier handling.

Figure 1   Figure 2

Coddled Eggs

Coddled eggs are just soft-cooked ones cooked until white is runny or fairly firm, as desired. Eggs are lowered carefully into gently boiling water, the pan covered (Fig. 2), removed from heat and the eggs allowed to stand in the hot water 2 to 4 minutes depending on the degree of cooking desired.

English Coddled Eggs

English Coddled Eggs . . . butter inside of coddler (Fig. 3). Break egg into it (Fig. 4). Add butter, salt and pepper. Screw on lid, lower into water (Fig. 5). Cook 10 minutes. Remove from water, remove lid and serve in china coddler.

Figure 3

Figure 4   Figure 5

Hard-Cooked Eggs I (Boiled)

Prepare as for Soft-Cooked Eggs I (this page) except let eggs stand in water 20 minutes. Cool at once in cold water.

Hard-Cooked Eggs II (Boiled)

Prepare as for Soft-Cooked Eggs II (this page) except keep water just below simmering stage about 20 minutes; cool in cold water immediately.

To Keep Eggs Yolks in Center of Hard-Cooked Eggs

Start cooking eggs in cold water (Hard-Cooked Eggs I); turn eggs constantly, but carefully, with long handled wooden spoon until water reaches the simmering stage.

To Prevent a Dark Ring Forming Around Yolk

Cook Hard-Cooked Eggs I or II as directed above. The dark ring will form when eggs are cooked too fast, too long, at too high a temperature or when they are not cooled immediately. Remove shells as soon as eggs are cold.

How To Shell Hard-Cooked Eggs

Peel eggs as soon as cold. Start at large end of egg and crack shell all over by tapping gently on a hard surface. Roll egg between palms of hands to loosen shell. Start peeling at large end of egg. Hold egg under running cold water while peeling if shell has a tendency to stick.

Why Do Some Hard-Cooked Eggs Have a Big Hollow at One End?

The hollow which appears at large end of a hard-cooked egg is an air pocket caused by a loss of moisture through the egg shell. The older the egg the larger the air hollow.

Only Egg Whites or Egg Yolks!

In order to prevent wasting surplus egg whites or egg yolks you can freeze them as directed on page 5.

If you don't wish to or can't freeze egg whites or yolks we have listed a variety of recipes at the beginning of the index on page 78. These recipes use one part of the egg or the other and should solve your surplus problem.

DECORATING EGGS

Fun with Eggs

Decorating eggs is fun. Handsomely decorated eggs can be enjoyed throughout the year. In addition to the pretty perky ones popular at Easter season potential artists with imagination and patience can turn empty egg shells into beautiful Christmas tree ornaments or art objects to mount on stands to enjoy the year around.

How To Decorate Eggs

Eggs To Use—Chicken, duck or goose eggs can all be used. Although hard-cooked eggs can be used it is best to empty egg shells so the decorated eggs can be enjoyed for days or weeks.

Figure 1   Figure 2

To Empty Egg Shells—Wash and dry eggs. Use a long slim needle; carefully pierce a hole through shell in ends of egg (Fig. 1). Press needle against edges of hole to widen slightly. Push needle into egg to break yolk. Hold one end of egg over a bowl. Blow into hole at opposite end (Fig. 2). Contents of shell will drain into bowl. Rinse shell in cold water; dry.

Decorations—Designs or decorations can be simple or complicated depending upon the skill of the decorator (Fig. 3 to 6). It is helpful to plan the decoration before starting. Colored tapes, stickers, stars, colored construction paper, tiny flowers, beads, gold or silver braids or designs, rick-rack, yarn, ribbon and bits of material can all be used for decorating eggs. Use glue to attach decorations to egg shell unless they have an adhesive backing. Use tweezers to attach tiny objects to eggs, it's easier.

Tinting Eggs—Use one of the commercial egg coloring kits; follow directions given on package.

A Few Easy Made Fancy Eggs

Funny Bunny—Use a white empty egg shell. Cut 2 long bunny ears (2½ inches long, ½ inch wide at center) out of pink construction paper. Draw face features at top of egg using a colored pencil with a fine point. Attach ears to back of head using glue or adhesive transparent tape. Make a tiny apron, vest or skirt out of cloth or construction paper and attach to bottom of egg. Set egg in tiny soufflé cup, small napkin ring, or paper ring made by gluing together ends of a strip of heavy paper.

Bunny Brummel—Prepare as for Funny Bunny except use a vest and glue a bit of pink-colored cotton to a pair of large bunny ears. Attach ears to egg and add pert cotton mustache.

Lady Lamb—Use a white empty egg shell. Cut 2 lamb ears (2 inches long, 1 inch wide at center) out of construction paper. Draw face features at top of egg using a colored pencil with a fine point. Crease lamb ears down center; glue onto egg at a horizontal angle. Add large fluff of cotton between ears.

Pretty Party Eggs—Tint empty egg shells. Decorate as your fancy directs with stripes of colored tapes or velvet ribbon, lace paper designs, lace, tiny beads, tiny flowers, bows, etc. Hang, group in a small dish or arrange on stands.

Figure 3

Figure 4   Figure 5

Figure 6

9

APPETIZERS

Chinese Egg Rolls

See photo at right

3 eggs
½ cup flour
1 tablespoon cornstarch
½ teaspoon salt
1 cup water
½ cup diced cooked chicken, pork, shrimp or crabmeat
¼ cup chopped bean sprouts
2 tablespoons finely chopped celery
2 tablespoons chopped mushrooms (fresh or canned)
  or water chestnuts
1 tablespoon finely chopped green onion
1½ teaspoons soy sauce

Beat 2 eggs slightly. Add flour, cornstarch, salt and water; beat with rotary beater until smooth. For each pancake pour 2 tablespoons batter into preheated lightly greased 6-inch fry pan. Tilt and rotate pan at once to allow batter to flow evenly over bottom of pan. Cook over medium heat until lightly browned on under-side and cooked on top side. Cook 1 side only. Prepare filling, combine next 5 ingredients; mix. Beat remaining egg; stir in soy sauce. Add to meat or seafood mixture; mix well. Spoon a rounded tablespoon of filling across center of each pancake; spread to within 1 inch of edges. Fold opposite 1 inch of sides of pancake over filling; roll up in opposite direction. Seal edge with beaten egg or leftover batter. Chill until ready to fry. Fry in hot fat (375°F.) 2 inches deep, until crisp and brown on all sides, about 3 minutes, turning as needed to brown evenly. Drain on paper toweling. Yield: 12 egg rolls, 4 servings.

Bacon 'N Egg Dip

1 can (6 ounce) tomato paste
½ cup salad dressing or mayonnaise
3 hard-cooked eggs, quartered
10 slices crisp cooked bacon, broken into 1-inch pieces
¼ medium green pepper, cut into 1-inch squares
¼ teaspoon salt
Dash of pepper
Dash of hot red pepper sauce

Combine ingredients in container of electric blender.* Whiz at low speed until smooth. Stop motor, as needed, during blending to scrape down sides of container with long handled rubber spatula. Serve with crisp crackers or Melba toast. Yield: About 2 cups.

*If blender is not available chop eggs and green pepper very fine and crumble bacon. Combine ingredients; mix well.

Deviled Ham and Egg Dip

2 cans (2¼ ounce) deviled ham
2 hard-cooked eggs, finely chopped
3 to 4 tablespoons salad dressing or mayonnaise
2 tablespoons finely chopped celery
¼ teaspoon curry powder
¼ teaspoon salt
Dash of pepper

Combine ingredients; mix well. Chill until serving time. Serve with favorite crackers, breads or toast. Yield: About 1¼ cups.

Salami Egg Dip

1 package (6 ounce) sliced hard salami (16 to 20 slices), finely chopped
2 hard-cooked eggs, finely chopped
½ cup salad dressing or mayonnaise
1 package (3 ounce) cream cheese, room temperature
½ teaspoon prepared horseradish

Combine ingredients; mix well. Chill. Serve with favorite crackers or Melba toast. Yield: About 2 cups.

Stuffed Cherry Peppers

2 hard-cooked eggs, finely chopped
2 tablespoons salad dressing or mayonnaise
2 tablespoons minced celery
1½ teaspoons chopped onion
1 teaspoon prepared mustard
1 teaspoon chopped pimiento
¼ teaspoon salt
¼ teaspoon Worcestershire sauce
About 18 cherry or sweet red pickled peppers

Combine first 8 ingredients; mix well. Cut stems from peppers; remove seeds and drain well. Fill peppers with about 2 teaspoonfuls of salad mixture. Yield: About 1½ dozen stuffed peppers.

CHERRY PEPPER APPETIZERS: Serve Stuffed Cherry Peppers on small rounds of white or whole wheat bread spread with softened cream cheese or a favorite cheese spread.

Zippy Egg Appetizers

2 hard-cooked eggs, finely chopped
1 tablespoon finely chopped pimiento
1½ tablespoons shredded Parmesan cheese
1 tablespoon minced parsley
¼ teaspoon dry mustard
¼ teaspoon salt
Salad dressing, mayonnaise or catsup
12 to 15 small Melba toast rounds or slices of party rye

Combine first 6 ingredients; mix well. Stir in just enough salad dressing, mayonnaise or catsup to make mixture a spreading consistency. Spread on toast or bread rounds. Arrange on baking sheet. Place in very hot oven (450°F.) 4 to 5 minutes or until heated. Yield: 12 to 15 appetizers.

Deviled Eggs

6 hard-cooked eggs, cut in half lengthwise
3 tablespoons salad dressing or mayonnaise
1 tablespoon milk or cream
1 tablespoon vinegar
2 teaspoons prepared mustard
¼ teaspoon sugar
¼ teaspoon salt
2 dashes hot pepper sauce

Remove yolks; save egg whites. Mash yolks until free of lumps. Add remaining ingredients; mix until smooth. Refill egg whites with egg yolk mixture. Garnish tops, if desired, with bits of pimiento, stuffed or black olive slices. Yield: 12 deviled egg halves, 6 servings.

VARIATIONS: Follow recipe for Deviled Eggs above and stir in the ingredients listed below:

ANCHOVY EGGS: Stir 1 or 2 tablespoons anchovy paste into egg yolk mixture.

CAVIAR EGGS: Stir 3 tablespoons well-drained caviar into egg yolk mixture.

CHEESE DEVILED EGGS: Stir ¼ cup shredded Cheddar cheese and 1 tablespoon well-drained sweet pickle relish into egg yolk mixture.

DEVILED HAM 'N EGGS: Stir ¼ cup finely chopped ham into egg yolk mixture.

DRIED BEEF EGGS: Stir 1½ tablespoons well-drained sweet pickle relish and ⅓ cup finely chopped dried beef into egg yolk mixture.

FISH OR SEAFOOD EGGS: Stir ¼ cup finely chopped cooked or canned shrimp, smoked fish, flaked crabmeat, tuna or salmon into egg mixture.

HERB EGGS: Stir ½ teaspoon chopped chives and ¼ teaspoon fines herbes blend into egg yolk mixture.

OLIVE EGGS: Stir 3 tablespoons chopped stuffed olives into egg yolk mixture.

Swiss Crêpe Appetizers

2 tablespoons butter or margarine
¼ cup flour
½ teaspoon salt
¼ teaspoon paprika
1 cup milk
1 cup diced process Swiss cheese
1 egg, beaten
About 4 dozen 4-inch crêpes
Egg wash*
2 cups fine corn flake crumbs
Cooking oil

Melt butter or margarine; stir in flour, salt and paprika. Add milk; cook stirring constantly until thickened. Add cheese; stir just until melted. Add a small amount of hot mixture to egg, stirring constantly. Return to hot mixture; cook stirring constantly until heated. Chill. For each appetizer spoon 1½ teaspoons cheese mixture in center of each crêpe; fold sides over filling and fasten with a wooden pick. Dip in egg wash and coat with crumbs. Fry in deep fat at 350°F., just until heated and browned, about 1 minute. Drain on absorbent paper. Serve hot. Yield: About 4 dozen appetizers.

*EGG WASH: Combine 2 eggs and ¼ cup milk; beat. Repeat if needed.

Crabmeat Filled Puffs

Cut tops from Tiny Appetizer Puffs (page 34). Fill bottoms with Crabmeat Salad Spread (page 64); replace tops.

Chicken Filled Puffs

Cut tops from Tiny Appetizer Puffs (page 34). Fill bottoms with Chicken Salad Spread (page 64); replace tops.

Egg Salad Filled Puffs

Cut tops from Tiny Appetizer Puffs (page 34). Fill bottoms with Egg Salad Sandwich Spread (page 64); replace tops.

Ham and Egg Salad Filled Puffs

Cut tops from Tiny Appetizer Puffs (page 34). Fill bottoms with Ham and Egg Salad Sandwich Spread (page 64); replace tops.

Salmon-Stuffed Eggs

8 hard-cooked eggs, cut in half lengthwise
⅓ cup salad dressing or mayonnaise
⅓ cup boned and finely flaked canned or smoked
    salmon
1 teaspoon Worcestershire sauce
¾ teaspoon prepared mustard
½ teaspoon salt
Dash of pepper

Remove yolks, save egg whites. Mash yolks until free of lumps. Combine salad dressing or mayonnaise, salmon, egg yolks and seasonings; mix well. Spoon mixture into egg whites. Chill until serving time. Garnish if desired with salmon pieces, olive slices or diced pimiento. Yield: 16 stuffed egg halves.

BEVERAGES

Egg Nog for Two

2 eggs
2 tablespoons sugar or equivalent amount of
    artificial sweetener
2 cups chilled milk or half and half (half milk,
    half cream)
1 teaspoon vanilla
Pinch of salt, optional
Pinch of nutmeg, optional

Combine ingredients in container of electric blender or
drink mixer. Whiz at low speed just until mixed. Pour
into chilled glasses. Yield: 2 large servings.

Egg Nog

4 eggs
¼ cup sugar
2 cups chilled milk
1½ teaspoons vanilla
¼ teaspoon salt
2 cups chilled half and half (half milk, half cream)
    or cream
1 cup whipped cream or dessert topping
Nutmeg

Combine first 5 ingredients in beater bowl or container
of electric blender; beat or whiz until well mixed. Pour
into chilled punch bowl. Stir in chilled half and half or
cream. Garnish with dollops of whipped cream or dessert topping and nutmeg. Yield: 5 cups, 8 to 10 servings.

VARIATIONS: Follow recipe for Egg Nog and change as
follows.

COFFEE NOG: Omit nutmeg and substitute 2 cups
chilled strong coffee for half and half. Yield: About 5
cups, 8 to 10 servings.

HOLIDAY NOG: Stir ½ to ⅔ cup brandy into eggnog
mixture before garnishing. Yield: About 5½ cups, 8 to
10 servings.

Hawaiian Nog

See photo page 15A

4 eggs, separated
¼ cup sugar
2 cups chilled milk
⅛ teaspoon salt
2 cups chilled pineapple-orange or pineapple-
    grapefruit juice
1 quart vanilla ice cream
3 slices canned pineapple
6 maraschino cherries

Beat egg yolks, sugar, milk and salt until light and
foamy. Stir pineapple juice into egg-milk mixture gradually. Pour into 6 tall glasses and top each with a scoop
of ice cream and garnish each glass with a half pineapple slice and maraschino cherry. Yield: 6 servings.

Party Egg Nog

6 eggs
1 cup sugar
¾ teaspoon salt
3 cups milk, scalded
3 cups chilled half and half (half milk, half cream) or
    light cream
1 cup chilled milk
4 teaspoons vanilla
1 tablespoon sherry
1½ cups whipped cream or dessert topping
Grated nutmeg

Beat eggs, sugar and salt slightly. Stir in 3 cups scalded
milk. Cook in top of double boiler over simmering water,
until mixture is thick enough to coat spoon. Chill well.
Stir in half and half or cream, chilled milk, vanilla and
sherry. Pour into chilled punch bowl; spoon whipped
cream or dessert topping onto egg nog. Sprinkle with
nutmeg. Yield: About 12 cups, 24 4-ounce servings.

BRANDY EGG NOG: Follow recipe for Party Egg Nog
above and substitute ½ cup brandy and ½ cup light
rum for 1 cup chilled milk. Yield: About 12 cups, 24
4-ounce servings.

Bouillon Nog

2 eggs
2 cups hot chicken or beef bouillon
⅛ teaspoon salt
Dash of hot red pepper sauce, optional

Whiz eggs in container of electric blender until light and
foamy. Add bouillon gradually through top opening with
motor running constantly during addition. Blend in
seasonings. Serve hot in mugs. Yield: About 2½ cups,
2 servings.

Root Beer Egg Shake

See photo page 15B

2 scoops (about 1 cup) vanilla ice cream
1 egg, beaten
1 can (12 ounce) root beer, chilled

Combine 1 scoop ice cream and egg; mix until smooth.
Pour into tall chilled soda glass; add root beer and stir
gently. Top with scoop of ice cream. Yield: About 1¾
cups, 1 serving.

Chocolate Egg Shake I

4 cups chilled milk or 2 cups milk and 2 cups half
    and half (half milk, half cream)
3 tablespoons sugar
3 to 4 tablespoons chocolate syrup, as desired
3 eggs, beaten slightly
1 teaspoon vanilla
¼ teaspoon salt
¼ cup whipped cream or dessert topping, optional

Combine first 6 ingredients; beat or shake until well
mixed. Serve plain or topped with whipped cream or
dessert topping. Yield: About 5 cups, 4 servings.

Chocolate Egg Shake II

2¼ cups chilled milk or half and half (half milk,
    half cream)
2 eggs
2 or 3 tablespoons chocolate syrup
2 tablespoons sugar
¾ teaspoon vanilla
¼ teaspoon salt
Crushed ice

Combine first 6 ingredients; beat well. Pour into tall
glasses packed with crushed ice. Yield: About 3 cups,
3 to 4 servings.

Egg 'N Honey Shake

2 eggs
2 cups chilled milk
¼ cup honey
1 teaspoon vanilla
Whipped cream or dessert topping, optional

Combine first 4 ingredients in beater bowl or container
of electric blender; beat or whiz until well mixed. Pour
into 4 chilled glasses. Garnish with dollops of whipped
cream or dessert topping, if desired. Yield: 4 servings.

Arctic Sparkle

See photo at right C

2 egg whites
¼ cup sugar
⅓ cup lemon juice
2 cups crushed ice
Chilled ginger ale

Shake ingredients, except ginger ale, in shaker. Pour
into 4 tall glasses; fill with ginger ale. Yield: 4 servings.

Dieter's Breakfast-in-a-Glass

2 eggs
2 cups chilled orange juice
⅔ cup non-fat dry milk solids
Artificial sweetener to taste

Combine first 3 ingredients in container of electric
blender or drink mixer. Whiz or beat until milk solids
are reconstituted. Pour into 2 glasses; let each person
stir in sweetener to taste. Yield: 2 servings.

Low Calorie Ice Cream Ginger Fizz

1⅓ cups drained canned dietetic fruit cocktail
2 eggs
2 to 4 scoops dietetic vanilla, New York or
    cherry ice cream
½ cup chilled low calorie ginger ale

Combine fruit cocktail, eggs and 2 scoops ice cream in
container of electric blender. Cover and whiz at low
speed until smooth. Stop motor; push ingredients into
blades with rubber spatula as needed. Pour an equal
amount into 2 tall glasses; stir in ginger ale. Serve as is
or top each glass with a scoop of ice cream, if desired.
Yield: 2 servings.

Orange Fizz

See photo at right D

3 egg whites
⅓ cup sugar or honey
3 cups chilled orange juice
¾ cup chilled lemon juice
1½ cups ice water
5 cups crushed ice

Beat egg whites until they form soft peaks. Gradually
add sugar or honey to egg whites and beat until stiff
and glossy. Add fruit juices and water; blend well. Fill
6 tall glasses with crushed ice; pour mixture over ice.
Garnish with mint sprigs. Yield: 6 servings.

Pink Cloud

See photo at right E

1 can (6 ounce) frozen pink fruit punch
    concentrate, defrosted
¾ cup ice water
¾ cup gin
2½ tablespoons sugar
2 medium-size egg whites
1½ cups chilled quinine water
Crushed ice
Fresh strawberries to garnish, if desired

Combine first 5 ingredients in container of electric
blender. Whiz at low speed a few seconds until well
mixed. Pour into pitcher; add quinine water and stir
gently. Fill tall glasses with crushed ice. Pour fruit mixture over ice; add straws and garnish each glass with
sliced or whole strawberries. Yield: 6 tall drinks.

Pineapple Egg Shake

4 eggs
2 cups chilled unsweetened pineapple juice
1 cup crushed ice
¼ cup sugar
2 tablespoons lemon juice
1 can (8¼ ounce) crushed pineapple, chilled
1 cup whipped cream or dessert topping

Combine first 5 ingredients in beater bowl or container
of electric blender; beat or whiz until well mixed. Stir
in crushed pineapple. Pour an equal amount into 6
chilled glasses. Top with whipped cream or dessert
topping. Yield: 6 servings.

Café de Belgique

1 cup (½ pint) whipping cream
½ teaspoon vanilla
2 small egg whites
Strong hot coffee
Granulated sugar

Whip cream until it forms soft peaks; stir in vanilla. Beat
egg whites until they form soft peaks; fold into whipped
cream. Fill 6 large or 8 small coffee cups or mugs ¼
full of cream mixture. Pour hot coffee into cups. Serve
at once with sugar, if desired. Yield: 6 to 8 servings.

Gourmet
INTERNATIONAL

E. Pink Cloud page 14

D. Orange Fizz page 14

B. Root Beer Egg Shake page 13

A. Hawaiian Nog page 13

C. Arctic Sparkle page 14

BREADS

Kolache

⅓ recipe Sweet Dough for Rolls and
   Coffee Cakes (this page)
⅓ cup thick raspberry or plum jam, apricot or
   peach preserves
2 tablespoons butter or margarine, melted
Confectioners' sugar

Divide dough into 12 equal portions. Shape each into a smooth ball; place 2 inches apart on greased baking sheet. Press a deep indentation in center of each ball with thumb. Fill hole with 1 teaspoon fruit jam or preserves. Cover; let stand in warm area until doubled in size. Bake in moderate oven (350°F.) 18 to 20 minutes or until done. Brush with butter or margarine; sprinkle with confectioners' sugar. Yield: 1 dozen rolls.

Sweet Dough for Rolls and Coffee Cakes

1¼ cups milk, scalded
½ cup butter, margarine or shortening
⅓ cup sugar
2 teaspoons salt
2 packages active dry yeast
½ cup warm water (110-115°F.)
3 eggs, beaten slightly.
7 cups (about) sifted flour

Combine milk, butter, margarine or shortening, sugar and salt in mixing bowl; cool to lukewarm. Soften yeast in warm water 5 minutes; stir until smooth. Add yeast, eggs and flour as needed to milk mixture to make a soft dough which can be handled. Turn onto lightly floured board and shape into a ball; knead until smooth and elastic. Place in buttered bowl; cover and set in warm area until double in size. Turn dough onto lightly floured board and make into the fancy rolls and coffee cake desired, see recipes that follow.

Butter Pecan Rolls

6 tablespoons butter or margarine, melted
⅔ cup (packed) brown sugar
3 tablespoons corn or pancake syrup
36 pecan halves
½ cup coarsely chopped pecans
⅓ recipe Sweet Dough for Rolls and
   Coffee Cakes (above)

Combine 3 tablespoons butter or margarine, ⅓ cup brown sugar and syrup; mix well. Place 3 pecan halves in bottoms of 12 well-buttered muffin cups. Top with an equal amount of sugar mixture. Roll dough into a 12-inch square on lightly floured board. Spread with remaining 3 tablespoons butter or margarine and ⅓ cup brown sugar. Sprinkle with chopped pecans. Roll up; cut into 12 slices 1 inch thick. Place slices, cut side up, in muffin cups. Cover with cloth or plastic film; place in warm area until double in size. Bake in moderate oven (350°F.) 20 minutes or until done. Turn pan upside down onto tray immediately after removing from oven. Let pan remain on rolls about 1 minute to let syrup run over sides of rolls. Yield: 1 dozen rolls.

Hot Cross Buns

1¼ cups warm water (110-115°F.)
2 packages active dry yeast
⅓ cup butter, margarine or shortening
½ cup sugar
3 eggs, beaten slightly
½ cup currants, seedless raisins or chopped mixed
   candied fruit
2½ teaspoons grated lemon rind
½ teaspoon cinnamon
1½ teaspoons salt
6½ cups (about) sifted flour
Confectioners' Sugar Icing (recipe follows)

Pour water into large mixing bowl; stir in yeast. Let stand 5 minutes; stir until dissolved. Stir in butter, margarine or shortening and sugar; stir until sugar dissolves. Stir in eggs. Add fruit, fruit rind, cinnamon, salt and flour as needed to make a soft dough. Turn onto floured board or pastry cloth; knead until smooth and elastic. Place in well-greased bowl; cover and place in warm area until double in size, about 1 hour. Turn onto floured board or pastry cloth; cut into 24 equal portions. Shape each piece into a smooth bun; space 2 inches apart on greased baking sheet. Cover loosely with plastic film and place in warm area until double in size. Bake in hot oven (425°F.) 15 to 20 minutes or until done and well-browned. Remove from oven; brush with melted butter, if desired, make a cross on top of each hot bun with Confectioners' Sugar Icing. Yield: 2 dozen buns.

Confectioners' Sugar Icing

¾ cup sifted confectioners' sugar
1 tablespoon hot water
½ teaspoon lemon extract

Combine ingredients; mix well. If too thick add water slowly as needed to make easy to spread icing.

Nut-Filled Butterhorns

Gourmet INTERNATIONAL

4 cups sifted flour
1¼ cups sugar
1 teaspoon salt
1 cup butter or margarine
2 packages active dry yeast
¼ cup warm water (110-115°F.)
½ cup dairy sour cream
4 eggs, separated
1 teaspoon vanilla
1 cup finely chopped pecans or walnuts
Confectioners' sugar

Combine flour, 2 tablespoons sugar, salt and butter or margarine in bowl. Blend butter or margarine into dry ingredients very well using fork or pastry blender. Dissolve yeast in warm water. Let stand 5 minutes; mix. Heat sour cream to lukewarm. Beat egg yolks slightly; stir in sour cream a small amount at a time. Stir in yeast and pour into dry ingredients; mix well. Cover with plastic film, aluminum foil or damp cloth. Chill 3 hours to overnight. Dough rises very little. Before rolling dough prepare filling. Beat room temperature egg whites until they form soft peaks. Add remaining 1 cup plus 2 tablespoons sugar gradually, beating constantly. Add vanilla; beat until whites form stiff peaks. Fold in nuts. Cut dough into 8 equal portions and shape each into a ball. Return to refrigerator. Roll one dough ball at a time on board sprinkled with confectioners' sugar. Roll dough in all directions from center into an 8-inch circle. Cut dough into 8 even pie-shaped wedges. Spread ⅛ of filling over dough. Roll up each wedge starting at wide end. Place on ungreased baking sheet. Repeat until all dough is shaped. Bake at once in a moderate oven (375°F.) 15 to 20 minutes or until golden brown. Remove from pan; cool on wire rack. Dust with confectioners' sugar before serving. Yield: 64 rolls.

Austrian Coffee Ring

4 cups sifted flour
1 teaspoon baking powder
1 teaspoon salt
1½ cups butter or margarine
2 cups sugar
6 eggs, separated
1 teaspoon grated lemon rind
1 cup milk
⅓ cup cocoa
⅓ cup water
Confectioners' sugar

Combine 2 cups flour, baking powder and salt; sift into bowl. Cream butter or margarine; add sugar gradually, creaming well after each addition. Add egg yolks and lemon rind and beat until light and fluffy. Blend in remaining 2 cups flour and milk alternately, mixing well after each addition. Beat egg whites until they hold soft peaks. Fold beaten whites and sifted flour mixture alternately into batter, blending well. Divide batter into 2 parts. Mix cocoa and water; stir into half of the batter. Spoon alternate layers of white and chocolate batter into 4 layers in greased and floured 10-inch spring form pan with tube. Bake in slow oven (325°F.) 1 hour and 15 minutes or until done. Cool in pan on wire rack 10 minutes. Remove from pan. Sprinkle with confectioners' sugar, if desired. Serve warm or cool. Yield: One 10-inch coffee cake.

Fruit Coffee Ring

3¾ cups sifted flour
3¼ teaspoons baking powder
1¼ teaspoons salt
1 cup butter or margarine, room temperature
1½ cups sugar
1½ teaspoons grated lemon rind
1½ teaspoons vanilla
3 eggs
⅓ cup milk
¾ cup chopped mixed candied fruit or currants
⅔ cup chopped walnuts or pecans

Combine 3 cups flour, baking powder and salt; sift. Cream ¾ cup butter or margarine; add 1 cup sugar gradually and cream until light and smooth. Beat in lemon rind and vanilla. Add eggs, one at a time, and beat well after each addition. Add dry ingredients and milk alternately a small amount at a time and mix well after each addition. Prepare crumb-fruit filling. Mix remaining ¾ cup flour and ½ cup sugar. Cut in remaining ¼ cup butter or margarine until mixture resembles fine crumbs. Stir in fruit and nuts. Starting with batter alternate layers of batter and crumbs in greased 10-inch tube pan, using ⅓ of each at a time. Bake in moderate oven (350°F.) 45 to 50 minutes or until done. Yield: One 10-inch cake, 4 inches high.

Fluffy French Toast

4 eggs, separated
3 tablespoons milk
⅛ teaspoon salt
2 tablespoons sugar
½ teaspoon vanilla
8 slices (½ to ¾ inch) day-old white bread
Favorite syrup or fruit sauce

Beat egg yolks, milk and salt until light and lemon colored. Beat egg whites until they form soft peaks. Add sugar, a small amount at a time, beating constantly during addition. Continue beating until egg whites form stiff peaks. Fold vanilla and egg yolks into egg whites. Dip bread slices into egg mixture. Arrange bread slices on well-buttered shallow pan. Bake in a very hot oven (450°F.) 5 to 8 minutes or until golden brown. Serve at once with favorite syrup or fruit sauce. Yield: 4 servings.

Oven-Fried French Toast

4 eggs
1 cup milk or half and half (half milk, half cream)
2 tablespoons sugar
¼ teaspoon salt
½ teaspoon vanilla
12 slices day-old bread (½ to ¾-inch thick)
1½ cups fine corn flake crumbs
Favorite syrup or fruit sauce

Combine first 5 ingredients in bowl; beat slightly. Dip bread slices into egg mixture quickly; drain and coat both sides with crumbs. Place on buttered 15 x 10 x 1-inch baking pans on baking sheets. Bake in hot oven (400°F.) 5 to 6 minutes; turn slices and bake until hot, crisp and browned, 6 to 8 minutes. Serve hot with favorite syrup or fruit sauce. Yield: 4 to 6 servings.

Braided Apricot Orange Coffee Cake

See photo at left

1 cup dried apricots, quartered
⅓ cup water
½ cup thick orange marmalade
⅓ cup sugar
2 teaspoons grated orange rind
⅓ recipe Sweet Dough for Rolls and
    Coffee Cakes (page 16)
Milk

Cook apricots in water in covered saucepan 5 minutes. Cover; let stand until cool. Mash. Stir in marmalade and 3 tablespoons sugar; cook over low heat until thick. Cool. Roll dough into a rectangle, 15 by 18 inches, on lightly floured board; transfer to greased baking sheet. Spread filling in a strip 3 inches wide down center of dough. Make cuts in dough 1 inch apart on each side of filling starting at outside edges and cutting to within ½ inch of filling. Starting at one end fold strips of dough from alternate sides across filling. Tuck ends of last strips under dough. Cover; place in warm area until double in size. Brush dough with milk and sprinkle with remaining sugar. Bake in moderate oven (350°F.) 30 minutes or until done. Remove from pan; cool on wire rack. Yield: One coffee cake, 15 inches long, about 12 servings.

Pecan Praline Coffee Cake

3½ cups sifted flour
1 cup (packed) brown sugar
3 teaspoons cinnamon
1½ teaspoons salt
1 cup butter or margarine
¾ cup finely chopped pecans
3 teaspoons baking powder
1 cup granulated sugar
1½ teaspoons vanilla
3 eggs
1 cup milk
1 cup seedless raisins or chopped mixed
    candied fruit

Combine ½ cup flour, brown sugar, cinnamon and ½ teaspoon salt; mix. Add ¾ cup butter or margarine; mix with pastry blender until mixture resembles coarse meal. Stir in pecans; set aside. Combine remaining 3 cups flour, baking powder, 1 teaspoon salt; sift. Cream remaining ¼ cup butter or margarine, granulated sugar and vanilla until light and fluffy. Add eggs one at a time and beat well after each addition. Add dry ingredients and milk to creamed mixture alternately, a small amount at a time, beating until smooth after each addition. Fold in raisins or candied fruit. Sprinkle ¼ of reserved crumb mixture evenly over bottom of well-greased 10-inch tube pan. Spread ½ of the batter over crumbs. Sprinkle ½ of remaining crumbs over batter. Cover with remaining batter and sprinkle with remaining crumbs. Bake in moderate oven (350°F.) 1 hour or until done. Cool in pan 10 minutes. Remove from pan. Serve warm or cooled. Yield: One 10-inch coffee cake, 10 to 12 servings.

Spoon Bread

2 cups water
1 cup yellow or white corn meal
1 cup milk
1¼ teaspoons salt
1 tablespoon baking powder
2 tablespoons butter or margarine, melted
4 eggs, beaten

Bring water to a rapid boil in 3-quart saucepan. Add corn meal to water in fine stream, stirring constantly. Stir in milk, salt, baking powder and butter or margarine. Add eggs and beat well. Pour into well-buttered 2-quart casserole. Bake in hot oven (400°F.) until just set, 40 to 45 minutes. Makes 8 servings.

Popovers

1 cup sifted flour
½ teaspoon salt
3 eggs
2 teaspoons butter or margarine, melted
1 cup milk

Combine flour and salt in small bowl; mix. Make a well in center of flour and add eggs, butter or margarine and milk. Beat until smooth. Fill well-greased 5-ounce custard cups or muffin pans half full. Bake in hot oven (400°F.) 35 to 40 minutes or until brown and crisp. Yield: 8 popovers.

HERB POPOVERS: Follow recipe for Popovers and add ¾ teaspoon fines herbes blend with dry ingredients.

PARMESAN POPOVERS: Follow recipe for Popovers and add ¼ cup grated Parmesan cheese with dry ingredients.

SPICE POPOVERS: Follow recipe for Popovers and add 1 tablespoon sugar, ¾ teaspoon cinnamon and ¼ teaspoon nutmeg with dry ingredients.

FIX-AHEAD POPOVERS: Prepare batter using recipe for Popovers 4 to 6 hours before serving time. Fill well-greased 5-ounce custard cups or muffin pans half full. Store in freezer. At serving time bake frozen batter in a hot oven (425°F.) until popovers are crisp and browned, 35 to 40 minutes.

Corn Meal Griddle Cakes

¼ cup sifted flour
1 tablespoon sugar
2 teaspoons baking powder
¾ teaspoon salt
½ teaspoon soda
1 cup yellow or white corn meal
3 eggs, beaten
1½ cups buttermilk
2 tablespoons butter or margarine, melted

Combine first 5 ingredients; sift into mixing bowl. Stir in corn meal. Add eggs, buttermilk and butter or margarine to dry ingredients. Stir until dry ingredients are moistened. For each pancake pour ¼ cup batter onto hot lightly greased griddle. Brown on first side; turn and brown second side. Serve with whipped butter and sorghum or pancake syrup. Excellent with pork sausage or ham. Yield: 12 pancakes, 4 servings.

Frenchie Brioches

See photo at right

2 packages active dry yeast
¼ cup warm water (110-115°F.)
1 cup butter or margarine
⅔ cup sugar
1½ teaspoons salt
¾ cup milk, scalded
7 cups (about) sifted flour
5 eggs
1 tablespoon cold water

Add yeast to water. Let stand 5 minutes; mix. Add butter or margarine, sugar and salt to milk; stir until sugar dissolves. Cool to lukewarm. Beat in 2 cups flour and yeast. Cover. Set in warm area until bubbly. Add 4 eggs; beat well. Add flour as needed to make a soft dough. Turn onto floured board or cloth; knead until smooth and elastic. Put in greased bowl, turn once and cover. Let rise until double in size, about 1½ hours. Punch down; divide dough in 24 equal pieces. Cut ⅓ of dough from each piece. Shape 24 large and 24 small balls. Place large balls in well-greased 2¾-inch muffin cups. Press an indentation in center of each with thumb. Press small balls into indentations. Cover and let rise in warm area until double in size, about 45 minutes. Mix remaining egg and 1 tablespoon water. Brush rolls with egg mixture. Bake in moderate oven (375°F.) 15 minutes or until well done and browned. Yield: 2 dozen brioche.

Gingerbread

⅔ cup molasses
½ cup sugar
½ cup butter or margarine
1 teaspoon ginger
1 teaspoon cinnamon
1 teaspoon baking soda
1 cup buttermilk
3 eggs, beaten
2 cups sifted flour

Warm molasses, sugar, butter or margarine, ginger and cinnamon. Dissolve soda in buttermilk; add to liquid ingredients. Add beaten eggs and sifted flour; mix well. Pour into a well-greased 13 x 9 x 1½-inch pan and bake in moderate oven (350°F.) 20 to 25 minutes or until done. Yield: 6 to 8 servings.

Favorite Pancakes

1½ cups sifted flour
3 tablespoons sugar
2 teaspoons baking powder
¾ teaspoon salt
3 eggs, beaten slightly
1⅔ cups milk
¼ cup melted shortening or cooking oil

Combine first 4 ingredients; sift into mixing bowl. Combine eggs, milk and shortening or oil; stir into dry ingredients. Mix just until dry ingredients are moistened. For each pancake pour ¼ cup batter onto hot, well-greased griddle. Brown on underside; turn and brown second side. Serve hot with butter or margarine and favorite syrup or fruit sauce. Yield: About 12 4-inch pancakes.

VARIATIONS: Follow recipe for Favorite Pancakes (this page) and change as follows:

BACON PANCAKES: Pan fry 6 slices bacon over low heat until crisp and lightly browned. Drain, cool and break into bits. Fold into batter. Serve with whipped butter or margarine and favorite pancake syrup. Yield: About 12 to 14 4-inch pancakes.

NUT PANCAKES: Fold ¾ cup coarsely chopped pecans or walnuts into batter. Serve with favorite syrup or sauce. Yield: About 14 4-inch pancakes.

BLUEBERRY PANCAKES: Fold ¾ cup fresh or well-drained defrosted frozen blueberries into batter. Serve with whipped butter and blueberry or pancake syrup. Yield: About 14 4-inch pancakes.

Quick Pancakes

1 cup pancake mix
1 tablespoon sugar
2 eggs
1 cup milk
2 tablespoons melted shortening or cooking oil

Combine pancake mix and sugar in mixing bowl. Stir in remaining ingredients; stir until smooth. Bake as directed for Favorite Pancakes (this page) or on package label. Yield: About 8 4-inch pancakes, 2 to 3 servings.

Quick Waffles

2 cups pancake mix
2 cups milk
3 eggs
½ cup melted shortening or cooking oil

Combine ingredients in mixing bowl. Beat just until batter is smooth. For each waffle pour ⅓ of batter onto 9-inch square waffle iron. Bake until done. Yield: 3 9-inch waffles, 12 4-inch waffle squares.

VARIATIONS: Follow recipe for Quick Waffles and change as follows:

ORANGE COCONUT WAFFLES: Stir ½ cup flaked coconut and 1½ teaspoons grated orange rind into batter just before baking. Serve with English Lemon Curd (page 65). Yield: 3 9-inch waffles, 12 4-inch waffle squares.

FRUIT WAFFLES: Fold in ½ cup of currants, seedless raisins, chopped pitted prunes or dates or dried apricots into batter before baking. Yield: About 3 9-inch waffles, 12 4-inch waffle squares.

Frenchie Brioches

CAKES AND TORTES

Old-Fashioned Burnt Sugar Cake

See photo at right

2 cups sugar
1 cup boiling water
3 cups sifted cake flour
3 teaspoons baking powder
½ teaspoon salt
1 cup butter or margarine, room temperature
1 teaspoon vanilla
4 eggs, separated

Spread 1 cup sugar in even layer over bottom of large heavy fry pan. Place over medium heat; allow sugar to turn a light golden color. Add boiling water ½ cup at a time. Be careful sugar will sputter, it's very hot! Stir until sugar is dissolved; cool. Save. Combine flour, baking powder and salt; sift. Cream butter or margarine, remaining 1 cup sugar and vanilla until light and fluffy. Add unbeaten egg yolks one at a time; beat well after each addition. Stir ½ of dry ingredients into creamed mixture. Add remaining dry ingredients and the caramel syrup alternately a small amount at a time; beat until smooth after each addition. Beat egg whites until they form soft peaks. Carefully fold egg whites into batter. Pour into three well-greased and floured 9-inch layer pans. Bake in moderate oven (350°F.) 20 to 25 minutes or until done. Cool 5 minutes; remove cake from pans and finish cooling on wire racks. Frost with caramel icing. Yield: Three 9-inch layers.

Gold Cake

2½ cups sifted cake flour
4 teaspoons baking powder
½ teaspoon salt
¾ cup butter or margarine, room temperature
1¼ cups sugar
1 teaspoon vanilla
8 egg yolks
¾ cup milk

Combine flour, baking powder and salt; sift. Cream butter or margarine, sugar and vanilla until light and fluffy. Beat egg yolks until light and fluffy. Blend into creamed mixture. Add dry ingredients and milk alternately to the creamed mixture. Beat just until smooth. Pour into 3 well-buttered and floured 9-inch layer pans. Bake in moderate oven (350°F.) 20 to 25 minutes or until done. Yield: Three 9-inch layers.

Spiced Prune Cake

2 cups sifted flour
3 teaspoons baking powder
¾ teaspoon cinnamon
¾ teaspoon cloves
½ teaspoon salt
¾ cup soft shortening
1 cup (packed) brown sugar
1 teaspoon vanilla
3 eggs, separated
1 cup cooked chopped pitted prunes
½ cup milk

Combine first 5 ingredients; sift into mixing bowl. Combine shortening, sugar and vanilla in bowl; beat until light. Add egg yolks and continue beating until fluffy. Stir in prunes. Add dry ingredients and milk, ½ at a time, and mix well after each addition. Beat egg whites until they form soft peaks. Fold into batter carefully. Turn into 2 well-greased 8-inch layer pans. Bake in moderate oven (350°F.) 25 to 30 minutes or until done. Cool in pans 5 minutes. Remove from pans and cool on wire rack. Put layers together and frost top and sides with Lemon Frosting (page 28). Yield: 2 layer, 8-inch cake.

Easy One-Bowl Yellow Cake

2 cups sifted flour
1½ cups sugar
3 teaspoons baking powder
1 teaspoon salt
½ cup soft shortening
2 teaspoons vanilla
1 cup milk
3 eggs, unbeaten

Combine first 4 ingredients; sift into bowl. Add shortening, vanilla and ⅔ cup milk. Beat at medium speed 2 minutes; scrape down bowl as needed. Add eggs and remaining milk. Beat at medium speed 2 minutes. Pour into 2 well-greased and floured 8-inch layer pans. Bake in moderate oven (350°F.) 30 to 35 minutes or until done. Cool cake in pans on racks 5 minutes; remove cake layers from pans and finish cooling on rack. Frost as desired. Yield: Two 8-inch layers.

White Cake

Follow recipe for Easy One-Bowl Yellow Cake (this page); substitute 4 egg whites (about ½ cup) for the 3 eggs called for.

Old-Fashioned Burnt Sugar Cake

Madeleines

See photo at left

1 cup sifted flour
½ teaspoon salt
4 eggs
1½ teaspoons vanilla
1½ teaspoons grated lemon rind
⅔ cup sugar
½ cup butter or margarine melted and cooled
Confectioners' sugar

Brush Madeleine pans well with melted butter or margarine and dust well with flour. Combine and sift flour and salt. Beat eggs, vanilla and lemon rind until light and lemon colored. Add sugar gradually and beat until thick and fluffy. Fold in dry ingredients. Add melted butter or margarine; mix carefully. Fill Madeleine pans ⅔ full. Bake in slow oven (325°F.) about 15 minutes or until done and lightly browned. Cool in pans on racks 2 to 3 minutes; removes cakes from pans and cool, shell side up, on rack. Before serving sprinkle with confectioners' sugar. Yield: 3 dozen cakes.

Spiced Carrot Cake

¾ cup plus 2 tablespoons fine dry bread crumbs
1 teaspoon baking powder
1 teaspoon salt
1 teaspoon cinnamon
1 teaspoon ginger
½ teaspoon mace
1½ cups finely ground blanched almonds
1 cup grated raw carrot
6 eggs, separated
1¼ cups sugar
1 teaspoon grated lemon rind
¼ cup lemon juice
Confectioners' Sugar Icing, if desired (recipe below)

Line bottom of buttered 9-inch spring form pan with waxed paper and butter paper. Sprinkle 2 tablespoons fine dry crumbs over bottom and sides of pan. Combine remaining ¾ cup crumbs, baking powder, salt and spices in mixing bowl; stir. Add almonds and carrot; mix well. Beat egg yolks until thick. Add 1 cup sugar, lemon rind and juice gradually and continue beating until thick and lemon colored. Fold into almond-carrot mixture. Beat egg whites until they hold soft peaks. Gradually beat in remaining ¼ cup sugar and continue beating until stiff and glossy. Fold into carrot mixture. Spoon into prepared pan. Bake in moderate oven (350°F.) 1 hour or until done. Cool in pan on wire rack. Remove from pan. Glaze with Confectioners' Sugar Icing, if desired. Store in air tight container. Flavor of cake improves with aging. Yield: One 9-inch cake.

Confectioners' Sugar Icing

1 cup sifted confectioners' sugar
1 tablespoon water
¼ teaspoon vanilla

Combine sugar, water and vanilla; mix until smooth. Add additional water if needed, a small amount at a time, until spreading consistency.

Angel Food Cake

1 cup sifted cake flour
1 cup sifted sugar
1¼ cups egg whites (10 to 12)
1¼ teaspoons cream of tartar
¼ teaspoon salt
1½ teaspoons vanilla
¼ teaspoon almond extract, optional

Measure and combine flour and ½ cup sugar; sift 3 times. Combine egg whites, cream of tartar, salt, vanilla and almond extract, if used, in large bowl. Beat until egg whites will hold soft peaks. Sprinkle remaining sugar, 2 tablespoons at a time, over egg whites and beat well after each addition. Continue beating until whites are stiff and glossy. Sift ¼ cup of flour-sugar mixture over the egg whites at a time and fold in with rubber scraper (about 15 strokes after each addition). Spoon into ungreased 10-inch tube pan. Bake in center of moderate oven (375°F.) 30 to 35 minutes or until done. Turn pan upside down on wire rack and cool thoroughly, 1 to 1¼ hours. Remove from pan and frost as desired. Yield: One 10-inch cake, 4 to 5 inches high.

Sponge Cake

1½ cups sifted flour
1½ cups sugar
1 teaspoon salt
8 eggs, separated
3 tablespoons cold water
2 tablespoons lemon juice
1½ teaspoons vanilla
1 teaspoon cream of tartar

Combine flour, ¾ cup sugar and salt; sift into bowl. Make a well in center of dry ingredients. Pour egg yolks, water, lemon juice and vanilla into well. Beat just until smooth. Beat egg whites and cream of tartar until they hold soft peaks. Add remaining ¾ cup sugar, 2 tablespoons at a time, and beat until stiff and glossy. Carefully fold egg yolk mixture into egg whites. Turn into ungreased 10-inch tube pan. Bake in moderate oven (350°F.) 50 to 55 minutes or until top will spring back when touched with finger. Turn pan upside down at once and allow cake to cool before removing from pan. Yield: One 10-inch tube cake, 5 inches high.

Rich Chocolate Cream

2 cups half and half (half milk, half cream) or cream
2 squares (1 ounce each) unsweetened chocolate,
    cut in small pieces
¾ cup sugar
⅓ cup flour
¾ teaspoon salt
6 egg yolks, beaten slightly
2 teaspoons vanilla

Scald half and half or cream and chocolate in heavy saucepan over low heat; mix. Combine sugar, flour and salt; mix. Add hot mixture gradually, stirring until smooth. Cook over low heat, stirring constantly until mixture thickens. Stir a small amount of hot mixture into egg yolks; stir into hot mixture and cook 2 or 3 minutes, stirring constantly. Stir in vanilla. Cool. Yield: 2¾ cups.

Chocolate Ice Cream Roll

¾ cup sifted confectioners' sugar
⅓ cup sifted flour
¼ cup cocoa
¾ teaspoon salt
6 eggs, separated
½ teaspoon cream of tartar
⅔ cup granulated sugar
1½ teaspoons vanilla
1 quart vanilla, chocolate or butter pecan ice cream,
    softened

Butter a 15 x 10 x 1-inch jelly roll pan; line with waxed paper and butter paper. Combine confectioners' sugar, flour, cocoa and salt; sift into bowl. Set aside. Beat egg whites and cream of tartar until they hold soft peaks. Add granulated sugar gradually and beat until egg whites hold stiff peaks. Beat egg yolks and vanilla until thick and lemon colored. Stir in reserved dry ingredients. Carefully fold egg yolk mixture into egg whites. Spread evenly into prepared pan. Bake in moderate oven (350°F.) 30 to 35 minutes or until done. Turn pan upside down on towel dusted with confectioners' sugar. Lift pan off cake; peel off paper. Trim off crisp edges. Beginning at narrow end roll cake up in towel. Cool. Unroll and spread ice cream evenly over cake. Reroll and freeze. When frozen wrap in plastic film or foil. Store in freezer. At serving time slice and serve plain or with favorite hot fudge sauce. Yield: 8 to 10 servings.

Jelly Roll

1 cup sifted flour
1 teaspoon baking powder
¼ teaspoon salt
3 eggs
1 cup sugar
¼ cup water
1½ teaspoons vanilla
Confectioners' sugar
1 cup thick preserves (red raspberry, strawberry
    or apricot)

Butter a 15 x 10 x 1-inch jelly roll pan; line with waxed paper and butter paper. Combine flour, baking powder and salt; sift. Beat eggs until very light and thick. Add sugar, 2 tablespoonfuls at a time, and continue beating until mixture is very thick. Carefully stir in water and vanilla, then fold in dry ingredients with an over and over motion. Do not overmix! Spread batter in an even layer in prepared pan. Bake in moderate oven (375°F.) 12 to 15 minutes or until cake will spring back when touched with a finger. Loosen edges of cake from pan; turn upside down onto towel well dusted with confectioners' sugar. Peel paper off of cake. Trim off ¼ inch of crust with sharp knife. Roll cake up in towel, starting at a narrow side. Cool. Remove towel. Unroll and spread preserves to within one inch of each edge. Reroll cake. Sprinkle with confectioners' sugar. Serve plain or with whipped cream or dessert topping. Yield: 8-10 servings.

Lemon Cake Roll

Prepare Jelly Roll (this page) and substitute 1 teaspoon grated lemon rind for vanilla and English Lemon Curd (page 65) or favorite lemon pudding (from mix, if desired) for preserves. Refrigerate until serving time. Dust with confectioners' sugar. Serve plain or with whipped cream or dessert topping. Yield: 8 to 10 servings.

Hungarian Chocolate Torte

5 eggs, separated
½ teaspoon salt
1 cup sifted confectioners' sugar
⅓ cup cocoa
1 teaspoon instant coffee powder
1½ teaspoons vanilla
1 package (3¼ ounce) vanilla pudding and pie
    filling (not instant)
2 cups half and half (half milk, half cream)
Chocolate Glaze (recipe page 28)

Line bottom of well-greased 15 x 10 x 1-inch baking pan with waxed paper and grease paper. Beat egg whites and salt until they hold soft peaks. Add sugar, 1 tablespoon at a time, and continue beating until stiff. Fold in cocoa and coffee. Beat egg yolks and vanilla until thick and lemon colored. Fold into cocoa mixture carefully. Spread over bottom of prepared pan. Bake in moderate oven (350°F.) 15 minutes or until done. Turn out on wire rack or cloth covered baking sheet. Remove paper at once and turn cake so top side is up. Cool. Cut in quarters crosswise. Prepare filling. Combine pudding and pie filling mix and half and half; cook as directed on package. Cool. Spread three layers of cake with filling. Stack layers; top with remaining layer. Chill. Spread top with glaze. Refrigerate until ready to serve. Yield: One torte about 10 x 3¾ x 2 inches; 8 to 10 servings.

Blitz Torte

Torte

1 cup sifted cake flour
1 teaspoon baking powder
½ teaspoon salt
½ cup butter or margarine, room temperature
1¼ cups sugar
1 teaspoon vanilla
4 eggs, separated
⅓ cup milk
½ cup blanched almonds, finely chopped

Filling

¼ cup sugar
1½ tablespoons cornstarch
1 cup milk
1 egg, beaten
1 teaspoon vanilla

Prepare torte: Combine flour, baking powder and salt; sift. Cream butter or margarine, ½ cup sugar and vanilla until light and fluffy. Add egg yolks, one at a time; beat well after each addition. Add dry ingredients and milk alternately a small amount at a time; mix well after each addition. Spread batter evenly into 2 well-greased and floured 8-inch layer pans. Beat egg whites until they form soft peaks. Add remaining ¾ cup sugar, 2 tablespoons at a time; beat until stiff and glossy after each addition. Spread in even layer on batter. Sprinkle with almonds. Bake in moderate oven (350°F.) about 30 minutes or until done. Cool in pans 5 minutes. Remove cakes from pans; cool well.

Prepare filling: Combine sugar and cornstarch in small saucepan; mix. Add milk and egg; mix well and cook over low heat, stirring constantly until thickened and smooth. Stir in vanilla. Cool; spread between 2 torte layers. Serve plain or topped with whipped cream or dessert topping, as desired. Yield: 8 to 10 servings.

Schaumtorte

Gourmet INTERNATIONAL

8 egg whites, room temperature
½ teaspoon cream of tartar
¼ teaspoon salt
2 cups very fine granulated sugar
2 teaspoons vinegar
2 teaspoons vanilla
3 cups sliced strawberries, peaches or whole
   red raspberries
½ cup sugar
¼ cup toasted slivered almonds
4 cups sweetened whipped cream or dessert topping

Draw a 9-inch circle on 3 sheets of heavy brown paper. Place each on a baking sheet and butter lightly. Combine egg whites, cream of tartar and salt in bowl. Beat until egg whites hold soft peaks. Add all but 2 tablespoons very fine sugar, 1 tablespoonful at a time, beating constantly until stiff and glossy. Add vinegar and vanilla and reserved 2 tablespoons sugar; continue beating until all sugar is dissolved. Spoon an equal amount of meringue on each circle spreading mixture to within ¼ inch of edge. Build up edges slightly. Bake in very slow oven (250°F.) 45 to 50 minutes or until a delicate beige color. Remove from oven; remove meringues from paper and return shells to oven to cool. At serving time place one shell on serving plate. Fold all but a few pieces of fruit, ½ cup sugar and nuts into whipped cream or dessert topping. Spoon ⅓ of mixture over meringue shell; cover with second meringue layer. Spoon ½ of remaining cream-fruit mixture on meringue and cover with third meringue layer. Top with remaining cream-fruit mixture and garnish with reserved fruit. Serve at once. Cut in wedges with cake breaker or sharp knife holding uncut torte in place with serving fork. Yield: 8 to 10 servings.

FROSTINGS FILLINGS AND CANDIES

Meringue

6 egg whites, room temperature
1½ teaspoons cream of tartar
½ teaspoon salt
1½ cups sugar
1 teaspoon vanilla

Draw a 9 or 10-inch circle on heavy brown paper. Place paper on baking sheet Combine egg whites, cream of tartar and salt; beat whites until they hold soft peaks. Add sugar, a tablespoon at a time, beating constantly until very stiff and glossy. Fold in vanilla. Spread meringue on paper circle to within ¼ inch of edge, mounding meringue up on outer edge. Bake in very slow oven (275°F.) 1 hour to 1¼ hours or until dry and a light beige color. Turn heat off and let meringue cool in oven. Remove from paper and fill with fruit, lemon, chocolate or butterscotch pudding and whipped cream or dessert topping, as desired. Yield: One 9 or 10-inch meringue.

Individual Meringues

Prepare as directed for Meringue (this page). Cover 2 baking sheets with heavy brown paper. Spoon meringue into 12 four-inch circles 2 inches apart or put through pastry bag with fluted tip. Hollow out center of each mound with back of spoon. Bake as directed for Meringue reducing baking time to 45 to 60 minutes. Yield: 12 individual meringues.

VARIATIONS: Follow recipe for Meringue (this page) and change as follows:

COFFEE MERINGUES: Mix 2 tablespoons instant coffee powder with sugar.

COCOA MERINGUES: Increase sugar to 1¾ cups and mix ¼ cup cocoa with last 4 tablespoons sugar. Fold sugar-cocoa mixture into beaten egg white mixture at the end.

Chocolate Glaze

2 tablespoons soft butter or margarine
1 cup sifted confectioners' sugar
⅓ cup cocoa
1 teaspoon vanilla
2 tablespoons boiling water, about

Combine first 4 ingredients. Add water as needed to make desired consistency, beating constantly. Yield: Enough for top of Hungarian Chocolate Torte page 26.

Chocolate-Rum Meringue Torte

6 egg whites, room temperature
½ teaspoon salt
½ teaspoon cream of tartar
1½ cups granulated sugar
½ cup (packed) light brown sugar
1½ teaspoons rum flavoring
Rich Chocolate Cream (recipe page 25)
Toasted slivered almonds

Turn three 8-inch layer pans, bottom side up; butter and flour bottoms. Combine egg whites, salt and cream of tartar; beat until they hold soft peaks. Add sugars, 3 tablespoons at a time, beating well after each addition. Beat until stiff and glossy. Blend in flavoring. Divide meringue in three equal portions; spread one portion evenly over bottom of each pan to within ½ inch of edges. Bake in very slow oven (275°F.) 1 hour. Turn heat off; cool meringues in oven. Remove meringues from pans carefully. Spread each meringue with ⅓ of chilled Rich Chocolate Cream and stack. Sprinkle with almonds. Refrigerate 4 hours or overnight. Yield: 8 to 12 servings.

7-Minute Frosting

1½ cups sugar
¼ cup water
2 tablespoons light corn syrup (or water)
⅛ teaspoon cream of tartar
⅛ teaspoon salt
2 egg whites
1 teaspoon vanilla or other flavoring

Combine first 6 ingredients in top of double boiler. Beat about 1 minute or until ingredients are well mixed. Place over gently boiling water; beat about 7 minutes or until frosting forms soft peaks and holds its shape. Remove from heat; continue beating until mixture is slightly cool and will spread without running. Stir in vanilla; spread onto cake layers. Yield: Frosts 2 layer 8-inch cake.

VARIATIONS: Follow recipe for 7-Minute Frosting and change as follows:

LEMON FROSTING: Substitute 3 tablespoons water and 2 tablespoons lemon juice for ⅓ cup water. Omit cream of tartar and substitute ¼ to ½ teaspoon grated lemon rind for vanilla.

CHOCOLATE SWIRL FROSTING: Gently fold 2 squares (1 ounce each) unsweetened chocolate, melted and cooled slightly, into prepared frosting. Important! Do not beat mixture.

PISTACHIO FROSTING: Add ½ teaspoon almond extract and green food color as needed to make frosting an attractive green color. Fold in ½ cup chopped toasted pistachio nuts.

MINT JULEP FROSTING: Substitute ¾ to 1 teaspoon mint extract for vanilla. Tint frosting a pretty green color with green food color. Fold in ½ to ⅔ cup chopped after dinner mints, chocolate mint patties or bits.

PEPPERMINT STICK FROSTING: Substitute ½ teaspoon peppermint extract for vanilla. Tint frosting a pretty peppermint pink with red food color. Fold in ¼ to ⅓ cup of coarsely crushed peppermint stick candy. Garnish frosted cake with additional chopped candy, melted unsweetened chocolate or chocolate sprinkles.

ORANGE FROSTING: Substitute 3 tablespoons water and 2 tablespoons orange juice for ⅓ cup water. Omit cream of tartar and substitute ¾ to 1 teaspoon shredded or grated orange rind for vanilla.

Never-Fail Fluffy White Frosting

2 egg whites
⅔ cup light corn syrup
⅓ cup sugar
⅛ teaspoon salt
1 teaspoon vanilla

Combine egg whites, syrup, sugar and salt in top of double boiler. Beat until ingredients are mixed. Place over boiling water and cook, beating constantly, 4 to 5 minutes or until mixture forms firm peaks. Remove from heat; beat about 1 minute longer. Add vanilla; mix well. Yield: Frosts 2 layer 8-inch cake.

FLUFFY BUTTERSCOTCH FROSTING: Prepare Never-Fail Fluffy White Frosting (at left) and substitute dark for light corn syrup and brown for granulated sugar.

Pastel Frostings

1¼ cups grape, mint or currant jelly or strawberry
   preserves
½ cup light corn syrup
2 egg whites
⅛ teaspoon salt

Heat jelly or preserves and corn syrup slowly in saucepan until jelly dissolves and mixture reaches the thread stage (230 to 234°F.). Combine egg whites and salt in bowl. Beat until egg whites hold soft peaks. Add hot syrup to egg whites in a fine stream beating constantly during addition. Continue beating until frosting forms firm peaks and spreads without running. Yield: Frosts 2 layer 8-inch cake.

3-Step Boiled Frosting

1½ cups granulated sugar
⅓ cup water
⅛ teaspoon cream of tartar
2 egg whites
1½ teaspoons vanilla extract

Combine sugar, water and cream of tartar in saucepan. Cook slowly until syrup reaches the soft ball stage (238°F.). While syrup is cooking beat egg whites until they form soft peaks. Pour ⅓ of the syrup, in a fine stream, over egg whites, beating constantly during addition. Beat at medium speed while syrup cooks to the firm ball stage (244°F.). Pour ½ of the remaining syrup, in fine stream, over egg white mixture, beating constantly. Beat at medium speed while last of syrup reaches the hard ball stage (250°F.). Pour last of syrup, in a fine stream, over egg white mixture, beating constantly. Continue beating until frosting is desired spreading consistency. Yield: Frosts 2 layer 8-inch cake.

Marzipan

See photo at left

2 egg whites
1 cup almond paste
½ teaspoon vanilla
1¼ cups sifted confectioners' sugar (or as needed
   to make mixture stiff enough to handle)

Beat egg whites until they hold stiff peaks. Add almond paste; mix well. Add vanilla and sugar; mix well. Shape into a ball and wrap in damp cloth, then in foil or plastic wrap. Refrigerate overnight. Color paste as desired with food colors and shape or mold into fruits and vegetables (pears, apples, peaches, potatoes, carrots and pumpkins). If desired, marzipan may be used for stuffing pitted dates and prunes. Yield: About 1½ cups.

Coconut Pecan Frosting

1 cup undiluted evaporated milk
1 cup sugar
3 egg yolks, beaten slightly
½ cup butter or margarine
1¼ teaspoons vanilla
1½ cups coarsely chopped pecans or walnuts
1⅓ cups flaked coconut

Combine first 4 ingredients; mix well. Cook slowly 10 to 12 minutes or until thickened, stirring constantly. Cool slightly; stir in vanilla, nuts and coconut. Stir until cool and a spreading consistency. Delicious on chocolate cake. Yield: About 2½ cups, enough for 2 8-inch layers.

Bohemian Icing

1 cup sugar
½ cup water
2 egg whites
1½ cups butter or margarine
2 egg yolks
1 teaspoon vanilla extract

Cook sugar and water together until syrup spins a long thread (234°F.). Beat egg whites until they form stiff peaks. Add syrup in a fine stream to egg whites, beating constantly until frosting forms stiff peaks. Cream butter or margarine, egg yolks and vanilla until light and fluffy. Fold butter mixture into egg white mixture; blend carefully. Yield: Frosts 2 layer 8 or 9-inch cake.

Mocha Frosting

3½ to 4 cups sifted confectioners' sugar
⅓ cup butter or margarine, room temperature
1½ tablespoons milk
¼ cup instant coffee powder
1½ teaspoons vanilla
¼ teaspoon salt
2 eggs
4½ squares (1 ounce each) unsweetened chocolate, melted and cooled slightly

Combine 3½ cups sugar, butter or margarine, milk, instant coffee, vanilla and salt; beat slowly until well blended. Add eggs; mix well. Blend in chocolate. If frosting is too soft, add confectioners' sugar until a spreading consistency. Yield: Frosts 2 layer 8 or 9-inch cake.

Chocolate Icing

2 cups sifted confectioners' sugar
⅓ cup cocoa
1 tablespoon soft shortening
1 egg
1 teaspoon vanilla
1 tablespoon boiling water, about

Combine first 5 ingredients in mixing bowl. Add water as needed to make desired spreading consistency, beating constantly. Yield: Frosts top of 13 x 9-inch cake or two 8-inch cake layers.

Pecan Divinity Fudge

3 cups sugar
⅔ cup light corn syrup
½ cup water
¼ teaspoon salt
2 egg whites (¼ cup)
1½ teaspoons vanilla
¾ cup coarsely chopped pecans
Pecan halves, optional

Combine first 4 ingredients in heavy saucepan. Cook over low heat until syrup reaches the hard ball stage (260°F.). Remove from heat. Beat egg whites until they hold stiff peaks. Add syrup in a fine stream to egg whites, beating constantly. Add vanilla and continue beating at high speed until mixture starts to stiffen and lose its gloss. Fold in pecans. Drop teaspoonfuls of candy onto buttered baking sheet or waxed paper and top each piece with a pecan half, if desired. Yield: About 64 candies.

Seafoam Frosting

1¼ cups (packed) brown sugar
¼ cup water
2 tablespoons light corn syrup
⅛ teaspoon salt
3 egg whites
1 teaspoon vanilla or ½ teaspoon maple flavoring

Combine sugar, water, syrup and salt in saucepan. Bring to a boil. Cook until syrup reaches the thread stage (230-234°F.). Beat egg whites until they hold soft peaks. Pour hot syrup in a fine stream into egg whites beating constantly during addition. Add vanilla or maple flavoring and continue beating until mixture forms stiff peaks. Yield: Frosts 2 layer 8-inch cake.

Nougat

2 cups sugar
½ cup light corn syrup
1 cup water
4 egg whites
¼ teaspoon salt
1 tablespoon butter, cut in small pieces
2 teaspoons vanilla
1½ cups pecan halves
1 cup candied cherries, cut in half

Combine 1 cup sugar, ¼ cup corn syrup and ½ cup water in small saucepan. Cook over low heat, stirring constantly until sugar dissolves. Cook, without stirring, to hard ball stage (250°F.). While syrup is heating beat egg whites and salt until they hold stiff peaks. Pour syrup in a very thin stream over egg whites, beating constantly at high speed. Let mixture stand. Cook remaining sugar, corn syrup and water in saucepan over low heat, stirring until sugar dissolves. Cook without stirring until syrup reaches the soft crack stage (280°F.). Add ⅓ of the hot mixture at a time to egg white mixture, beating vigorously with wooden spoon. Add butter. Continue beating until mixture is very thick. Stir in vanilla, pecans and cherries; mix well. Spoon into well-buttered 8 x 8 x 2-inch baking pan. Cool slightly; refrigerate until firm. Cut in squares. Yield: About 36 pieces.

COOKIES

Swiss Almond Squares

6 eggs
1 cup granulated sugar
¼ teaspoon salt
6 squares (1 ounce each) semi-sweet chocolate,
    melted and cooled
1 teaspoon cinnamon
½ teaspoon ground allspice
½ teaspoon ground cloves
1 teaspoon grated lemon rind
2 teaspoons lemon juice
1½ cups (about ½ pound) blanched almonds,
    finely ground or chopped
1 cup unsifted flour
2 cups sifted confectioners' sugar

Separate eggs; save 3 egg whites for frosting. Beat egg yolks and granulated sugar until light and fluffy. Beat 3 egg whites and ⅛ teaspoon salt until they hold stiff peaks; fold into egg yolk mixture. Fold chocolate, spices, lemon rind and 1 teaspoon lemon juice into egg mixture. Fold in almonds and flour. Spread evenly into well-buttered and floured 15 x 10 x 1-inch jelly roll pan. Prepare frosting. Beat remaining 3 egg whites, 1 teaspoon lemon juice and ⅛ teaspoon salt until egg whites form stiff peaks. Fold in confectioners' sugar, ⅓ at a time. Spread evenly over chocolate mixture. Bake in moderate oven (375°F.) 20 to 25 minutes or until frosting is golden brown and a cake tester inserted into chocolate layer comes out clean. Loosen edges with sharp knife while warm and cut into bars with a wet knife. Cool; remove from pan with wide spatula. Yield: About 6 dozen cookies.

Frosted Squares

Gourmet INTERNATIONAL

See photo page 32B

½ cup shortening
1 cup granulated sugar
2 teaspoons vanilla
2 eggs
2 tablespoons water
1⅔ cups sifted flour
1¼ teaspoons baking powder
½ teaspoon salt
2 egg whites
¾ cup (packed) light brown sugar
¾ cup chopped pecans or walnuts

Cream shortening, granulated sugar, 1½ teaspoons vanilla and 2 eggs until light and fluffy. Add water; mix well. Sift flour, baking powder and salt together; stir into creamed mixture and mix well. Spread over bottom of well-greased 15 x 10 x 1-inch jelly roll pan. Beat egg whites and vanilla until they hold soft peaks. Add brown sugar, 2 tablespoons at a time, and continue beating until stiff and glossy. Fold in ¼ cup nuts. Spread over cookie mixture. Sprinkle remaining nuts over meringue. Bake in slow oven (325°F.) 30 minutes or until done. Cool and cut in squares. Yield: 35 2-inch squares.

Nutty Date Bars

1 cup sifted flour
1 teaspoon baking powder
½ teaspoon salt
3 eggs
1 cup sugar
1 teaspoon vanilla
1½ cups chopped pitted dates
1½ cups coarsely chopped pecans or walnuts
Confectioners' sugar, optional

Combine flour, baking powder and salt; sift. Combine eggs, sugar and vanilla and beat until light and lemon colored. Stir in dry ingredients, dates and nuts. Spread into greased baking pan (13 x 9 x 2-inches). Bake in slow oven (325°F.) 30 minutes or until done. Cool. Cut into bars; serve plain or dust with confectioners' sugar. Yield: About 36 bars 1 x 3 inches.

Nut Brownies

Gourmet INTERNATIONAL

¾ cup sifted flour
¾ teaspoon baking powder
½ teaspoon salt
⅓ cup butter or margarine, room temperature
1 cup sugar
2 eggs
1½ teaspoons vanilla
3 squares (1 ounce each) unsweetened chocolate,
    melted and cooled
1 cup coarsely chopped pecan halves

Combine flour, baking powder and salt; sift. Beat butter or margarine, sugar, eggs and vanilla until very creamy; stir in chocolate and dry ingredients. Fold in pecans. Turn into greased 8 x 8 x 2-inch pan. Bake in moderate oven (350°F.) 25 to 30 minutes or until done. Cool on rack. Serve plain or frost with favorite chocolate frosting. Yield: 16 brownies.

Molasses Raisin Cookies

3 cups sifted flour
3 teaspoons baking powder
2 teaspoons cinnamon
1½ teaspoons ginger
½ teaspoon nutmeg
½ teaspoon salt
1 cup seedless raisins
1½ cups whole wheat flakes
1 cup soft shortening
1 cup (packed) brown sugar
2 eggs
¾ cup molasses

Combine first 6 ingredients; sift into mixing bowl. Stir in raisins and cereal. Beat shortening, sugar and eggs until light and fluffy. Stir in molasses. Add dry ingredients and mix well. Drop rounded tablespoonfuls of dough onto lightly greased baking sheets. Bake in moderate oven (350°F.) 12 to 15 minutes or until done and lightly browned. Remove from pan at once; cool on wire rack. Yield: About 4½ dozen cookies.

Coconut Kisses

See photo at right A

2 egg whites
⅛ teaspoon cream of tartar
¼ teaspoon salt
1 cup sugar
1½ teaspoons vanilla
2 cans (3½ ounce) or 2 cups flaked coconut
½ cup chopped mixed candied fruit or candied
    cherries

Combine egg whites, cream of tartar and salt. Beat
until foamy. Add sugar, 1 tablespoonful at a time; beating constantly during addition. Continue beating until
sugar dissolves and mixture forms stiff peaks. Add
vanilla. Fold in coconut and fruit. Drop teaspoonfuls of
mixture onto buttered baking sheet. Bake in slow oven
(300°F.) about 20 minutes or until dry and crisp.
Loosen from pan with spatula at once. Transfer to wire
racks to cool. Yield: 24 to 32 kisses.

Chinese Chews

See photo at right C

¾ cup sifted flour
1 teaspoon baking powder
¼ teaspoon salt
2 eggs
1 cup sugar
1 teaspoon vanilla
1 cup finely chopped pitted dates
1 cup coarsely chopped walnuts or pecans
Confectioners' sugar

Combine first 3 ingredients; sift. Beat eggs, sugar and
vanilla until light and lemon colored. Stir in dry ingredients. Blend in dates and nuts. Spread evenly over
bottom of greased 9 x 9 x 2-inch pan. Bake in slow
oven (325°F.) 40 minutes or until done. Sift confectioners' sugar over warm cookies before cutting into
bars or cool until lukewarm, cut in bars and roll in
confectioners' sugar. Yield: About 25 bars.

Corn Flake Meringues

See photo at right D

3 egg whites
⅛ teaspoon cream of tartar
¼ teaspoon salt
¾ cup sugar
1 teaspoon vanilla
1¼ cups corn flakes, regular or pre-sweetened
½ cup flaked coconut

Beat egg whites slightly. Add cream of tartar and salt;
beat until whites hold soft peaks. Add sugar gradually,
2 tablespoonfuls at a time; beat until glossy after each
addition. Add vanilla; beat until mixture holds stiff
peaks. Fold cereal and coconut into egg white mixture.
Drop rounded tablespoonfuls of mixture 2 inches apart
on ungreased brown paper on baking sheet. Bake in
slow oven (275°F.) 45 minutes to 1 hour or until firm
and lightly browned. Cool away from drafts. Yield:
About 2¼ dozen.

A. Coconut Kisses   B. Coconut Squares page 31
C. Chinese Chews   D. Corn Flake Meringues

DESSERTS

Custard

2 cups milk
⅓ cup sugar
¼ teaspoon salt
1½ teaspoons vanilla
3 eggs
Nutmeg, optional

Combine first 4 ingredients; stir until sugar is dissolved. Add eggs; beat slightly. Fill 5 or 6 (5-ounce) custard cups to within ½-inch of top. Sprinkle nutmeg over tops, if desired. Arrange cups in shallow baking pan. Place on oven rack and fill pan to 1-inch depth with hot water. Bake in slow oven (325°F.) 25 to 30 minutes or until firm. A knife blade inserted in center will come out clean when custard is done. Serve warm or chilled, plain or with favorite fruit or dessert sauce. Yield: 5 to 6 servings.

VARIATIONS: Follow recipe for Custard and change as suggested below:

SPEEDY-COOK CUSTARD: Instead of baking custards in oven, cover each dish with aluminum foil; arrange on rack in a heavy fry pan or Dutch oven. Add hot water as needed to fill the pan to bottom of rack. Cover; cook custards until they test done, 15 to 20 minutes. A knife point inserted in center of custard will come out clean when done.

TOFFEE CUSTARD: Omit nutmeg and 5 minutes before end of baking time sprinkle finely crushed plain or chocolate covered toffee over custards.

TOASTED COCONUT CUSTARD: Omit nutmeg and 10 minutes before end of baking time sprinkle tops of custards with lightly toasted flaked coconut.

COFFEE CUSTARD: Add 1½ to 2 teaspoons instant coffee powder to milk; reduce vanilla to 1 teaspoon and omit nutmeg. Serve warm or chilled, plain or with whipped cream, chocolate or marshmallow sauce.

Crème Brûlée

Follow Custard recipe (this page) and substitute whipping cream or half and half (half milk, half cream) for milk. Increase eggs to 4 and omit nutmeg. Bake in buttered individual soufflé dishes or custard cups. Just before serving top each well chilled custard with 2 teaspoons brown sugar. Pack dishes in pan of crushed ice. Broil 4 inches from heat just until sugar melts and caramelizes. Serve at once. Yield: 5 to 6 servings.

French Vanilla Ice Cream

2 cups half and half (half milk, half cream)
¾ cup sugar
1 tablespoon flour
¼ teaspoon salt
4 to 6 egg yolks (or 4 eggs)
2 tablespoons vanilla
2 cups chilled whipping cream

For Freezing in Refrigerator

Scald half and half in heavy saucepan over low heat or in top of double boiler. Don't allow to boil! Mix together sugar, flour and salt; stir into half and half. Beat egg yolks (or eggs) slightly; pour a small amount of the hot half and half into eggs, stirring constantly. Stir egg mixture slowly into remaining hot half and half. Cook until smooth and thickened, stirring constantly. Stir in vanilla. Cool, stirring often. Chill. Beat whipping cream until it holds soft peaks; fold into chilled custard. Pour into 2 refrigerator trays or a 1-quart loaf pan. Set freezing unit at coldest point; freeze until firm (about 3 hours). Yield: 1 quart.

For Freezing in Manual or Electric Ice Cream Freezer

Prepare as directed above except do not whip cream. Stir cream into custard. Put dasher in freezer can and ice cream mixture. Cover. Freeze as directed by manufacturer. Ice cream is best when packed and left to stand 3 to 4 hours to mellow. Yield: 1 quart. Double recipe if desired for ½ gallon of ice cream.

Pots de Crème Café

4 teaspoons instant coffee powder
2 cups half and half (half milk, half cream), scalded
6 egg yolks
⅔ cup sugar
⅛ teaspoon salt
1 cup sweetened whipped cream or dessert topping

Stir coffee into hot half and half. Combine egg yolks, sugar and salt; beat until very light and lemon colored. Stir half and half into eggs slowly. Pour into 6 petits pots. Place in a pan of hot water; bake in slow oven (300°F.) 35 to 40 minutes or until set. A knife inserted in the center comes out clean when done. Chill. To serve, top desserts with a dollop of whipped cream or dessert topping. Yield: 6 servings.

Tiny Appetizer Puffs

Prepare Cream Puff dough (page 36). Drop teaspoonfuls of dough 2 inches apart onto ungreased baking sheets. Bake in hot oven (400°F.) 20 to 25 minutes or until puffed, light golden brown and dry. Remove from baking sheets; cool on wire rack away from drafts. Split and fill with favorite meat, seafood, poultry, egg salad, sandwich spread or cheese; replace tops and serve. Yield: About 36 puffs.

Eclairs

Put Cream Puff dough (page 36) through pastry tube or paper cone with opening 1 inch wide. Make 4-inch strips 2 inches apart on ungreased baking sheets. If no pastry bag is available spoon strips of dough 1 inch wide and 4 inches long on baking sheets. Bake in hot oven (425°F.) 15 minutes then reduce to slow oven (325°F.) for 25 minutes or until puffed, lightly browned and dry. Turn heat off. Remove eclairs from baking sheets. Split in half lengthwise; return to oven to dry out. Cool. Frost tops with Chocolate Glaze (page 28). Just before serving fill bottom halves with ice cream, cream filling or vanilla pudding, replace tops. Yield: About 1 dozen eclairs.

Swiss Chocolate Torte

1 cup sifted flour
1 teaspoon baking powder
½ teaspoon salt
2 packages (4 ounce each) German sweet chocolate
½ cup butter or margarine
1 cup sugar
5 eggs, separated
1 teaspoon vanilla
½ teaspoon rum extract
Confectioners' sugar, whipped cream or ice cream, as desired

Line bottom of greased 9-inch spring form pan with waxed paper and grease paper. Sift flour, baking powder and salt together. Combine chocolate and butter or margarine in heavy saucepan; place over very low heat until melted, stirring to blend. Add ¾ cup sugar; stir until smooth and sugar melted. Pour into mixing bowl. Beat in egg yolks, one at a time, beating well after each addition. Stir in flavorings. Stir in flour mixture. Beat egg whites until they hold soft peaks. Gradually add remaining ¼ cup sugar and continue beating until whites are stiff and glossy. Carefully fold ⅓ of egg white mixture into chocolate mixture, then fold in remaining egg white mixture. Pour batter into prepared pan. Bake in moderate oven (350°F.) 40 to 45 minutes or until done. (This torte has a crusty top that cracks and tends to sink slightly in the center but has great flavor). Cool on wire rack 10 minutes. Remove sides of pan and cool thoroughly. Remove waxed paper. Sprinkle with confectioners' sugar or serve with whipped cream or ice cream. Yield: One 9-inch torte.

Baked Chocolate Nut Fondue

2 squares (1 ounce each) unsweetened chocolate
1 cup milk
1 tablespoon butter or margarine
¾ cup sugar
½ teaspoon salt
3 eggs, separated
1 cup soft torn crust free bread crumbs
1½ teaspoons vanilla
⅓ cup chopped pecans or walnuts
Whipped cream or dessert topping

Combine chocolate, milk, and butter or margarine in heavy saucepan; cook over low heat, stirring constantly, until chocolate is melted. Remove from heat. Beat egg yolks, ½ cup sugar, salt and vanilla until light and lemon colored. Stir a small amount of hot chocolate mixture into eggs then stir into remaining chocolate mixture. Fold in crumbs and nuts. Beat egg whites until they hold stiff peaks. Add remaining ¼ cup sugar gradually and beat until stiff and glossy. Fold into chocolate mixture. Pour into buttered 1½ quart casserole. Bake in moderate oven (300°F.) 40 to 45 minutes or until puffed and firm. Serve warm with whipped cream or dessert topping. Yield: 6 servings.

Bread Pudding

5 eggs, slightly beaten
¾ cup sugar
1½ teaspoons vanilla
¼ teaspoon salt
4 cups soft crust-free bread cubes (½ to ¾ inch)
4 cups milk, scalded

Combine eggs, sugar, vanilla and salt; beat slowly until ingredients are mixed. Spread bread cubes in buttered shallow 1½-quart baking dish. Add milk to egg mixture slowly, stirring constantly. Pour over bread cubes. Set in pan of hot water. Bake in moderate oven (350°F.) about 1 hour, or until set. A knife inserted in center will come out clean when done. Serve warm or cold with cream or whipped cream. Yield: 6 servings.

BREAD PUDDING VARIATIONS: Follow recipe for Bread Pudding and change as follows:

APPLE RAISIN BREAD PUDDING: Sprinkle ¾ cup seedless raisins and 1 cup peeled diced apple over bread cubes. Add ¾ teaspoon cinnamon and ½ teaspoon nutmeg to eggs before beating. Bake in 2-quart shallow casserole.

PRUNE BREAD PUDDING: Spread ¾ cup cooked pitted prunes, cut in quarters, over bread cubes. Add 1 tablespoon grated orange rind to milk. Bake in 2-quart shallow casserole.

Frozen Orange Parfait

See photo below

Gourmet INTERNATIONAL

1¼ cups sugar
⅓ cup water
6 egg yolks
¼ teaspoon salt
½ cup orange juice
1½ tablespoons grated orange rind
⅓ cup orange liqueur (Grand Marnier or Cointreau)
½ pint (1 cup) whipping cream, whipped
Whipped cream for garnish
Fresh or candied orange sections for garnish

Combine sugar and water in heavy saucepan; bring to boil and simmer 5 minutes. Remove from heat. Place egg yolks and salt in a second heavy saucepan. With beater, beat until thick and lemon colored. Gradually add hot sugar syrup in a thin stream, beating constantly. Place over low heat and continue beating until very thick. Remove from heat; set in pan of ice water and continue beating until cold. Stir in orange juice, rind and liqueur. Fold in whipped cream. Pour into foil-lined loaf pan, 8½ x 4½ x 2⅝-inches. Freeze. Unmold on platter; remove foil. Decorate with whipped cream and orange sections. Yield: 6 to 8 servings.

Spanish Caramel Flan

1 cup sugar
3 tablespoons boiling water
3 cups milk
4 eggs
1½ teaspoons vanilla
¼ teaspoon salt
Sweetened whipped cream or dessert topping, optional

Spread ¾ cup sugar evenly over bottom of heavy fry pan. Place over moderate heat and heat slowly until sugar melts and turns a light caramel color, stirring constantly. Add boiling water slowly, stirring constantly. Stir until sugar is dissolved. Pour into 1-quart casserole. Tilt and turn casserole until bottom is evenly coated with syrup. Set aside. Combine milk, eggs, remaining ¼ cup sugar, vanilla and salt; beat slightly. Pour into casserole over syrup. Place casserole in pan of hot water. Bake in moderate oven (350°F.) 40 to 45 minutes or until done. A knife inserted in center of casserole will come out clean when done. Cool then chill in refrigerator. Loosen edge of custard from casserole with point of knife. Turn upside down on a serving plate with an edge. Before lifting casserole let caramel sauce drain from bottom of custard onto plate. Remove casserole. Serve with whipped cream or dessert topping, if desired. Yield: 6 servings.

Frozen Orange Parfait

Cream Puffs

1 cup water
½ cup butter or margarine
¼ teaspoon salt
1 cup sifted flour
4 eggs

Combine first 3 ingredients in heavy saucepan. Bring to a boil. Add flour, all at once, and stir vigorously with wooden spoon until mixture leaves the sides of the pan and forms a smooth ball. Remove from heat; add eggs, one at a time, beating well after each addition. Continue beating until mixture is smooth and velvety. Drop slightly rounded tablespoonfuls of dough 2 inches apart on ungreased baking sheet. Bake in hot oven (400°F.) 45 to 50 minutes or until puffed, golden brown and dry. Remove from pan; cool on wire racks away from drafts. Cut in half and fill with whipped cream or dessert topping; replace top and sprinkle with confectioners' sugar, or fill as suggested at right. Yield: About 1 dozen large puffs.

CREAM PUFF VARIATIONS: Prepare Cream Puffs (this page) and fill with one of the following:

CHOCOLATE PEPPERMINT ICE CREAM PUFFS: *(See photo below)* Fill bottom halves of Cream Puffs with peppermint ice cream. Replace tops; serve with favorite hot fudge or chocolate sauce.

STRAWBERRY, RASPBERRY OR PEACH ICE CREAM PUFFS: Fill Cream Puffs with vanilla, New York or French ice cream; serve with defrosted frozen strawberries, raspberries or peaches. If preferred, sweetened sliced fresh strawberries, peaches or sweetened raspberries may be substituted for frozen ones.

DOUBLE CHOCOLATE ICE CREAM PUFFS: Fill Cream Puffs with chocolate chip or chocolate ice cream and serve with hot fudge or chocolate sauce.

LEMONY CREAM PUFFS: Fill Cream Puffs with favorite lemon pudding (made from mix, if desired). Replace tops and dust with confectioners' sugar.

DREAMY CREAM PUFFS: Fill Cream Puffs with whipped cream-candy filling. To prepare filling fold chopped peanut brittle or peppermint stick candy, as desired, into whipped cream or dessert topping. Serve with chocolate sauce or dust with confectioners' sugar.

Quick Chocolate Dessert

5 eggs, separated
½ teaspoon salt
1 cup sifted confectioners' sugar
⅓ cup unsweetened cocoa
1½ teaspoons vanilla
3 cups whipped cream or dessert topping
Chocolate curls or chopped nuts

Butter and line a 15 x 10 x 1-inch jelly roll pan with waxed paper; butter paper. Beat egg whites and salt just until they hold soft peaks. Add sugar, 1 tablespoon at a time, beating well after each addition. Fold in cocoa. Beat egg yolks and vanilla until thick and fluffy. Fold yolks into egg white-cocoa mixture. Spread batter evenly in prepared pan. Bake in moderate oven (350°F.) 20 minutes or until done. Turn out on clean towel dusted with confectioners' sugar. Remove paper from cake. Cool 15 minutes; cut in half lengthwise and crosswise. Spread ¼ of whipped cream or topping on each cake layer. Stack layers and top with chocolate curls or chopped nuts. Refrigerate until serving time. Yield: 8 to 10 servings.

Orange-Lemon Cake Pudding

¼ cup butter or margarine, room temperature
1 cup sugar
4 eggs, separated
¼ cup sifted flour
3 tablespoons orange juice
2 tablespoons lemon juice
2 teaspoons grated orange rind
½ teaspoon grated lemon rind
1 cup milk
¼ teaspoon salt

Cream butter or margarine and sugar until well mixed. Add egg yolks and beat until light and smooth. Stir in flour, fruit juices and rinds, milk and salt. Beat egg whites until they form soft peaks. Fold into batter. Pour into an 8 x 8 x 2-inch pan. Set in pan of hot water. Bake in moderate oven (350°F.) 45 minutes or until done. Serve warm or chilled spooned into dessert dishes. Yield: About 6 servings.

Brockel Torte Dessert

6 eggs
1⅔ cups sifted confectioners' sugar
1 cup chopped pitted dates
1 cup coarsely chopped walnuts
½ cup fine bread or corn flake crumbs
2 teaspoons baking powder
½ teaspoon salt
Whipped cream or dessert topping

Beat eggs until very light. Add sugar gradually, beating well after each addition. Combine remaining ingredients in bowl; mix well. Add egg mixture; mix well but carefully. Pour into well-greased and floured 9 x 9 x 2-inch baking pan. Bake in moderate oven (350°F.) 25 to 30 minutes or until browned and done. Cool in pan 5 minutes, turn out and cool on rack. Cut into squares. Serve warm or cold topped with whipped cream or dessert topping. Yield: 9 to 12 servings.

Fruity Cheese Cake with Almond Crumb Crust

Crust

⅓ cup butter or margarine, melted
⅛ teaspoon almond extract
1¾ cups fine rich butter cookie crumbs
⅓ cup sugar
⅓ cup very finely chopped or ground blanched almonds

Filling

2 packages (8 ounce each) cream cheese, room temperature
4 eggs
2 teaspoons vanilla
1 teaspoon grated lemon rind
⅔ cup sugar
2 tablespoons flour
½ teaspoon salt

Sauce

3 tablespoons sugar
1 tablespoon cornstarch
1 package (10 ounce) frozen red raspberries, strawberries or sliced peaches in syrup, defrosted
⅓ cup toasted slivered almonds

PREPARE CRUST: Combine butter or margarine and almond extract; mix into crumbs and sugar with pastry blender. Stir in almonds. Press mixture evenly over bottom and up 1¾ inches on sides of buttered 9-inch spring form pan. Chill well.

PREPARE FILLING. Beat cream cheese and 1 egg until smooth. Add remaining eggs, one at a time, beating well after each addition. Add vanilla and lemon rind. Combine and mix sugar, flour and salt. Add to egg mixture gradually; mix well. Spoon into crust; bake in moderate oven (350°F.) 40 minutes or until firm. Cool in pan then refrigerate.

PREPARE SAUCE. Combine sugar and cornstarch. Drain syrup from defrosted fruit and stir into sugar-cornstarch mixture. Cook, stirring constantly, until thick and clear. Add fruit and heat. Spoon over top of cheese cake; sprinkle almonds over fruit. Chill 2 to 3 hours before serving time. Yield: One 9-inch cheese cake, 12 to 16 servings.

Mocha Mousse

2 envelopes (2 tablespoons) unflavored gelatin
½ cup cold water
6 egg yolks, beaten slightly
1 cup sugar
1½ cups strong coffee
½ teaspoon salt
1½ pints (3 cups) whipping cream
1 teaspoon vanilla

Soften gelatin in cold water; let stand 5 minutes. Combine egg yolks, ¾ cup sugar and coffee; beat slightly. Cook in heavy saucepan over low heat, stirring constantly, until mixture is thick enough to coat the spoon. Add gelatin; stir until dissolved. Cool until mixture is consistency of thick syrup, stirring often. Whip cream; fold in remaining ¼ cup sugar and vanilla. Fold whipped cream into coffee mixture. Pour into oiled 2-quart mold. Chill until firm. Unmold. Garnish, if desired, with additional whipped cream and serve with favorite chocolate sauce. Yield: 8 to 10 servings.

Baked Alaska

To Serve or Freeze

½ of a 9 x 9 x 2-inch baked yellow, white or
    chocolate cake layer or 1 loaf 8½ x 3½ x 2½-inch
    commercial pound cake
3 pints strawberry, chocolate or appropriate
    ice cream for cake
6 egg whites
¼ teaspoon cream of tartar
¼ teaspoon salt
1 cup sugar
Strawberry or chocolate sauce or appropriate
    sundae sauce

Trim crusts from top and sides of cake; cut cake lengthwise into 3 even slices. Arrange slices on large baking sheet; freeze. Cut each pint of ice cream in 3 even slices, starting on wide side and cutting top to bottom. Arrange 3 ice cream slices, side by side, on each frozen cake slice. Return to freezer to harden. Cut each slice of cake and ice cream into 4 servings. Place in freezer while preparing meringue. Beat egg whites, cream of tartar and salt together until they hold soft peaks. Add sugar, 1 tablespoon at a time, beating until mixture is stiff and glossy. Frost each cake completely with meringue sealing meringue to cake. Place on baking sheet in extremely hot oven (500°F.) 3 to 5 minutes or until attractively browned. Serve at once with favorite strawberry, chocolate or other sundae sauce. If preferred, put browned Alaskas in freezer at once, unwrapped; freeze. Wrap when frozen. Plan to use in 2 or 3 days. Yield: 12 servings.

Super Strawberry Pancakes

8 baked Favorite Pancakes (page 20)
⅓ cup soft butter or margarine
¼ cup (packed) brown sugar
2 cups cleaned fresh strawberries, halved
¼ cup granulated sugar
1 cup whipped cream or dessert topping

Spread tops of baked pancakes with butter or margarine; sprinkle with brown sugar. Stack pancakes and keep warm. Combine strawberries and granulated sugar and mash well. To serve, cut stacked pancakes into 4 wedges; spoon strawberries over each wedge and serve with whipped cream or dessert topping. Yield: 4 servings.

Norwegian Crown Dessert Torte

Cake
1½ cups sifted flour
1 teaspoon baking powder
6 egg yolks
½ cup milk
1 cup sugar
3 egg whites
1 teaspoon vanilla
½ teaspoon salt

Filling
½ cup sugar
3 tablespoons flour
2 tablespoons cornstarch
¼ teaspoon salt
2 eggs
2 cups milk
2 tablespoons butter or margarine
1 teaspoon vanilla
¼ teaspoon rum extract

Meringue
3 egg whites
¼ teaspoon cream of tartar
¼ teaspoon salt
6 tablespoons sugar
¼ cup sliced blanched almonds
Assorted fruits (apricots, maraschino cherries,
    peach slices and pineapple chunks)

MAKE CAKE. Sift flour and baking powder together Beat egg yolks, milk and ½ cup sugar 5 to 10 minutes until thick and lemon colored. Fold in flour mixture, ⅓ at a time. Beat egg whites, vanilla and salt until they hold soft peaks. Gradually add remaining ½ cup sugar and continue beating until stiff and glossy. Fold carefully into egg yolk mixture. Pour batter into 2 greased and floured 9-inch cake layer pans. Bake in moderate oven (350°F.) 15 to 20 minutes or until done. Remove from pans at once and cool on wire racks.

MAKE FILLING. Combine sugar, flour, cornstarch and salt in heavy saucepan; mix. Add eggs and milk; beat well. Cook stirring constantly until thickened and smooth. Add butter or margarine and extracts; stir. Cool, stirring occasionally. Assemble torte. Cut cake layers in half crosswise. Spread three layers with filling, stack and top with fourth layer. Chill.

MAKE MERINGUE. Beat egg whites, cream of tartar and salt until they hold soft peaks. Gradually add sugar and continue beating until stiff and glossy. Spread on top and sides of chilled torte and sprinkle with sliced almonds. Bake in moderate oven (350°F.) 10 to 12 minutes or until meringue is lightly browned. Arrange well-drained fruits on top to resemble jewels in a crown. Yield: One 9-inch torte.

PIES

Lemon Chess Pie

4 eggs
1½ cups sugar
⅓ cup lemon juice
1 teaspoon grated lemon rind
¼ cup flour
¼ teaspoon salt
¼ cup butter or margarine, melted
9-inch unbaked pastry shell

Beat eggs until lemon colored. Gradually beat in sugar, lemon juice and rind. Stir in flour, salt and butter or margarine. Pour into pastry shell. Bake in moderate oven (350°F.) 45 minutes or until done. Cool. Yield: One 9-inch pie.

Pecan Pie

3 eggs, slightly beaten
1 cup dark corn syrup
½ cup sugar
2 tablespoons butter or margarine, melted
1 teaspoon vanilla
¼ teaspoon salt
1 cup pecan halves
9-inch unbaked pastry shell

Combine eggs, syrup, sugar, butter or margarine, vanilla and salt; mix well. Stir in pecans. Pour into unbaked shell. Bake in hot oven (400°F.) 10 minutes; reduce heat to moderate (350°F.) and continue baking 35 to 40 minutes or until filling is firm. Cool. Serve plain or with whipped cream, if desired. Yield: One 9-inch pie.

MACADAMIA NUT PIE: Follow recipe for Pecan Pie and substitute coarsely chopped macadamia nuts for pecans. Yield: One 9-inch pie.

CHOCOLATE PECAN PIE: Follow recipe for Pecan Pie and add 2 squares (1 ounce each) unsweetened chocolate, melted. Yield: One 9-inch pie.

Custard Pie

4 eggs, slightly beaten
½ cup sugar
½ teaspoon salt
1 teaspoon vanilla
2½ cups milk, scalded
9-inch unbaked pastry shell
Nutmeg

Combine first 4 ingredients in mixing bowl. Gradually add scalded milk, stirring constantly. Pour into pastry shell. Sprinkle with nutmeg. Bake in moderate oven (350°F.) 35 to 40 minutes or until filling is set. A metal knife inserted in center of filling comes out clean when done. Cool. Yield: One 9-inch pie.

MINCEMEAT CUSTARD PIE: Follow recipe for Custard Pie. Omit nutmeg. Spread 1 cup well-drained prepared mincemeat evenly over bottom of unbaked shell. Pour custard mixture carefully over mincemeat. Yield: One 9-inch pie.

COCONUT CUSTARD PIE: Follow recipe for Custard Pie. Omit nutmeg. Sprinkle ½ cup flaked coconut over unbaked custard filling. Yield: One 9-inch pie.

Rhubarb Custard Pie

1½ cups sugar
2 tablespoons flour
¼ teaspoon salt
3 cups (½-inch) sliced rhubarb
9-inch unbaked pastry shell with high fluted rim
1 cup half and half (half milk, half cream)
3 eggs, slightly beaten

Combine 1 cup sugar, flour and salt; toss with rhubarb until pieces are evenly coated. Let stand about 15 minutes; spoon into pastry shell. Combine half and half, eggs and ½ cup sugar; pour over rhubarb. Bake in hot oven (400°F.) for 15 minutes; reduce heat to moderate (350°F.) and bake 50 minutes longer or until custard is set and rhubarb is tender. Chill. Yield: One 9-inch pie.

Pumpkin Pie

1½ cups canned pumpkin
½ cup granulated sugar
½ cup (packed) brown sugar
1½ teaspoons cinnamon
¾ teaspoon ginger
½ teaspoon cloves
½ teaspoon nutmeg
½ teaspoon salt
3 eggs, slightly beaten
1 can (13 ounce) evaporated milk, undiluted (1⅔ cups)
9-inch unbaked pastry shell
Whipped cream, optional

Combine pumpkin, sugars, spices and salt; mix well. Blend in eggs and milk. Pour into pastry shell. Bake in hot oven (425°F.) 10 minutes; reduce heat to moderate (350°F.) continue baking 35 to 40 minutes or until knife inserted in center comes out clean. Cool. Serve with whipped cream, if desired. Yield: One 9-inch pie.

Lemon Cream Pie

Lemon Cream Pie

See photo at left

1¼ cups sugar
⅓ cup cornstarch
½ teaspoon salt
2 cups milk
3 egg yolks
⅓ cup lemon juice
1½ to 2 teaspoons grated lemon rind
1½ tablespoons butter or margarine
9-inch baked pastry shell
Meringue Topping (below)

Mix sugar, cornstarch and salt in heavy saucepan. Add milk; stir until smooth. Cook stirring constantly until thickened. Remove from heat. Beat egg yolks. Stir a small amount of hot mixture into beaten egg yolks. Return to hot mixture, stirring constantly. Stir in lemon juice and rind. Cook 2 or 3 minutes stirring constantly. Remove from heat. Stir in butter or margarine. Cool slightly; pour into baked pastry shell. Cover with meringue and brown. Chill. Yield: One 9-inch pie.

Meringue Topping

For Lemon, Butterscotch and Chocolate Pies

3 egg whites
¼ teaspoon cream of tartar
⅛ teaspoon salt
6 tablespoons sugar
1 teaspoon vanilla or ½ teaspoon lemon extract

Beat egg whites until foamy. Add cream of tartar and salt and beat until the egg whites hold soft peaks. Gradually add sugar and continue beating until stiff and glossy. Add vanilla or lemon extract; beat. Spread on top of filled pie, sealing meringue to crust edges. Place in moderate oven (350°F.) 12 to 15 minutes or until lightly browned. Yield: Meringue for one 9-inch pie.

Lemon Cake-Custard Pie

1 cup sugar
¼ cup flour
½ teaspoon salt
1 tablespoon grated lemon rind
¼ cup butter or margarine, melted
4 eggs, separated
1 cup milk
¼ cup lemon juice
9-inch unbaked pastry shell with very high fluted rim
2 tablespoons sliced blanched almonds

Combine ¾ cup sugar, flour, salt and lemon rind. Blend in butter or margarine. Add egg yolks and beat well. Stir in milk; gradually stir in lemon juice. Beat egg whites until they hold soft peaks. Gradually add remaining ¼ cup sugar and continue beating until stiff and glossy. Fold egg whites into yolk mixture. Pour into unbaked pastry shell; sprinkle top with almonds. Bake in hot oven (400°F.) 10 minutes; reduce heat to slow oven (325°F.) and continue baking 20 to 25 minutes or until filling is set. Serve slightly warm or cool. Yield: One 9-inch pie.

Chocolate Chiffon Pie

¾ cup granulated sugar
1 envelope (1 tablespoon) unflavored gelatin
½ teaspoon salt
4 eggs, separated
2 cups milk
2 squares (1 ounce each) unsweetened chocolate
2 teaspoons vanilla
9-inch baked pastry shell

Combine ½ cup sugar, gelatin and salt; stir. Add egg yolks and milk; beat slightly. Stir in chocolate. Cook, stirring constantly, until thickened. Beat to blend chocolate evenly. Blend in vanilla. Cool until mixture begins to set, stirring occasionally. Beat egg whites until they hold soft peaks. Gradually add remaining ¼ cup sugar and continue beating until stiff and glossy. Beat chocolate mixture until smooth. Fold in egg white mixture. Spoon into shell. Chill until firm. Garnish with whipped cream and chocolate curls, if desired. Yield: One 9-inch pie.

MOCHA CHIFFON PIE: Follow recipe for Chocolate Chiffon Pie. Reduce chocolate to 1 square (1 ounce) and add 2 to 3 tablespoons instant coffee powder to milk.

Fluffy Lemon Pie

1 envelope (1 tablespoon) unflavored gelatin
1 cup sugar
½ teaspoon salt
5 eggs, separated
½ cup water
½ cup lemon juice
2 teaspoons grated lemon rind
Yellow food color as desired
9-inch baked pastry shell or graham cracker crust
1½ cups sweetened whipped cream
Thin lemon slices, optional

Combine gelatin, ½ cup sugar and salt in heavy saucepan; mix. Add egg yolks, water and lemon juice; beat slightly. Cook, stirring constantly, until gelatin is dissolved and mixture coats spoon. Add lemon rind and yellow color to tint a light lemon yellow color. Chill until mixture begins to set, stirring occasionally. Beat egg whites until they hold soft peaks. Gradually add remaining ½ cup sugar and continue beating until stiff and glossy. Beat gelatin mixture well. Fold in egg white mixture. Spoon into shell. Chill until firm. Garnish with whipped cream and thin lemon slices, if desired. Yield: One 9-inch pie.

Banana Butterscotch Pie

See photo at right

¾ cup (packed) brown sugar
⅓ cup flour
½ teaspoon salt
2 cups milk
3 eggs
1 tablespoon butter or margarine
1½ teaspoons vanilla
9-inch baked pastry shell or crumb crust
2 ripe bananas, sliced
1 to 1½ cups sweetened whipped cream, optional

Mix sugar, flour and salt in heavy saucepan. Add milk; stir until smooth. Cook, stirring constantly until thickened. Remove from heat. Stir a small amount of hot mixture into beaten eggs. Return to remaining hot mixture. Cook 1 minute, stirring constantly. Remove from heat. Stir in butter or margarine and vanilla. Cool thoroughly, stirring occasionally. Cover bottom of pastry shell or crust with small amount of filling. Make alternate layers of sliced bananas and butterscotch filling ending with filling. Chill. Serve plain or topped with whipped cream, if desired. Yield: One 9-inch pie.

Lemon Angel Pie

Meringue Crust

4 egg whites, room temperature
1 teaspoon vanilla
¼ teaspoon cream of tartar
¼ teaspoon salt
1 cup sugar

Filling

4 egg yolks
½ cup sugar
¼ cup lemon juice
1 tablespoon grated lemon rind
½ pint (1 cup) whipping cream, whipped

PREPARE CRUST. Beat egg whites until foamy. Add vanilla, cream of tartar and salt. Beat until egg whites hold soft peaks. Gradually add sugar, a tablespoonful at a time, and continue beating until very stiff and glossy. Spread meringue evenly over bottom and up sides of buttered 9-inch pie pan to form shell. Bake in very slow oven (275°F.) about 1 hour or until shell is very lightly browned, crisp and dry. Cool.
PREPARE FILLING. Combine egg yolks, sugar and lemon juice in heavy saucepan; mix. Cook, stirring constantly, until thick. Stir in lemon rind. Chill, stirring often. Fold whipped cream into chilled lemon mixture. Spoon into cooled crust. Refrigerate several hours or overnight before serving. Yield: One 9-inch pie.

STRAWBERRY ANGEL PIE: Follow recipe for Lemon Angel Pie, using crust only. Substitute strawberry filling for lemon filling. To make strawberry filling, dissolve 1 package (3 ounce) strawberry flavored gelatin in ¾ cup boiling water. Chill until gelatin begins to set. Fold in 1 package (10 ounce) frozen strawberries, defrosted, and ½ pint (1 cup) whipped cream, whipped. Chill until mixture begins to mound. Spoon into cooled crust. Refrigerate. Yield: One 9-inch pie.

CHOCOLATE ANGEL PIE: Follow recipe for Lemon Angel Pie, using crust only. Substitute chocolate for lemon filling called for. To prepare chocolate filling combine 1 package (6 ounce) semi-sweet chocolate pieces and ¼ cup water or coffee in heavy saucepan. Place over low heat stirring until chocolate is melted; stir until smooth. Cool. Whip ½ pint (1 cup) whipping cream until stiff. Fold in 2 tablespoons sugar and 1 teaspoon vanilla. Fold in chocolate mixture. Spoon into cooled crust. Refrigerate. Yield: One 9-inch pie.

Orange Coconut Pie

1½ cups sugar
¼ cup cornstarch
1½ cups orange juice
4 eggs, separated
2 tablespoons butter or margarine
1 tablespoon grated orange rind
1 can (3½ ounce) flaked coconut
¼ teaspoon cream of tartar
¼ teaspoon salt
9-inch baked pastry shell

Combine 1 cup sugar and cornstarch; mix. Add orange juice and egg yolks; beat. Cook, stirring constantly, until thickened. Add butter or margarine and orange rind; stir until butter or margarine is melted. Save 2 tablespoons coconut for meringue; stir remaining coconut into orange mixture. Let cool while preparing meringue. Beat egg whites until foamy. Add cream of tartar and salt; beat until they hold soft peaks. Gradually add remaining ½ cup sugar and continue beating until stiff and glossy. Fold ⅓ of meringue into orange mixture. Spoon filling into baked shell. Top with remaining meringue, sealing to edges of crust. Sprinkle with remaining coconut. Bake in moderate oven (350°F.) 12 to 15 minutes or until meringue is lightly browned. Cool. Yield: One 9-inch pie.

Key Lime Pie

2 eggs, slightly beaten
1 can (15 ounce) sweetened condensed milk (1⅓ cups)
½ cup lime juice
1 teaspoon grated lime rind
¼ teaspoon salt
Green food coloring
9-inch baked pastry shell or crumb crust
Whipped cream, optional

Combine first 5 ingredients. Beat with rotary or electric beater until mixture thickens. Add green color as desired to tint mixture a pale green. Pour into pie shell or crust. Bake in moderate oven (350°F.) 10 minutes or until filling is set. Cool. Serve with whipped cream, if desired. Yield: One 9-inch pie.

KEY LIME PIE WITH SOUR CREAM TOPPING: Follow recipe for Key Lime Pie. While pie is heating, mix ½ pint (1 cup) dairy sour cream, ¼ cup sugar and ⅛ teaspoon salt. Spread evenly over top of warm filling. Increase oven heat to hot (400°F.). Return pie to oven, 5 minutes or until sour cream is set. Yield: One 9-inch pie.

ENTRÉES

Hearty Sportsmans' Breakfast

⅓ cup butter or margarine
3 medium-size potatoes, peeled and diced (¼-inch)
2 small onions, sliced and separated into rings
1 teaspoon salt
⅛ teaspoon pepper
2 tablespoons chopped parsley
8 eggs
3 tablespoons half and half (half milk, half cream)
   or milk
½ cup crisp bacon bits, optional

Melt butter or margarine in large heavy fry pan over moderate heat. Add potatoes; cover and cook slowly until a light golden brown. Add onion rings; cook until tender. Season with salt and pepper. Stir in chopped parsley. While potatoes are cooking beat eggs slightly; stir in cream and pour over potato mixture. Cover and continue cooking over low heat until eggs begin to set, stirring carefully during cooking. Serve plain or topped with bacon bits. Yield: 4 to 6 servings.

Brunch Egg Scramble

12 eggs
1 teaspoon salt
¼ teaspoon marjoram
⅛ teaspoon pepper
¼ cup butter or margarine
2 cans (4 ounce each) sliced mushrooms, drained
1 cup shredded process American cheese (about
   ¼ pound)

Combine eggs, salt, marjoram and pepper; beat slightly; set aside. Melt butter or margarine in large heavy fry pan over moderate heat. Add egg mixture, mushrooms and cheese. Cook over low heat to firmness desired, stirring carefully. Yield: 6 to 8 servings.

Fisherman's Wharf Scrambled Eggs

6 eggs
3 tablespoons white wine
3 tablespoons grated or shredded Parmesan cheese
¾ teaspoon salt
⅛ teaspoon pepper
Dash of hot pepper sauce
3 tablespoons butter, margarine or olive oil
½ pound ground beef
1 package (10 ounce) frozen leaf spinach, defrosted
Hot buttered Italian or French bread, optional

Combine first 6 ingredients; beat slightly and set aside. Heat butter, margarine or olive oil in large heavy fry pan over low heat. Add meat and cook, stirring constantly until meat is broken up into chunks and is grey in color. Add spinach; cover pan and cook spinach until limp, 4 to 5 minutes. Add eggs and cook to doneness desired, stirring frequently. Serve with hot buttered Italian or French bread. Yield: 4 servings.

Chili Scrambled Eggs

3 tablespoons bacon drippings
½ cup chopped green pepper
⅓ cup sliced green onion
1 cup diced (¾-inch) raw tomato
1 teaspoon chili powder
1¼ teaspoons salt
8 eggs
¼ cup milk or half and half (half milk, half cream)
1 pound bacon, cooked crisp and drained

Heat 2 tablespoons bacon drippings in large saucepan. Add green pepper and onion; cook over low heat until vegetables are tender, not brown. Turn off heat; add tomatoes. Sprinkle with chili powder and ¼ teaspoon salt; mix carefully. Cover and let stand while eggs are cooking. Combine eggs, milk or half and half and remaining 1 teaspoon salt; stir slightly. Heat remaining bacon drippings in fry pan; add egg mixture and cook over low heat, stirring gently from bottom of pan as egg mixture starts to set. Cook to desired degree of doneness. Turn onto heated serving platter, spoon vegetables over eggs. Serve with crisp bacon. Yield: 4 to 6 servings.

Swiss Scrambled Eggs

6 eggs
⅓ cup milk or half and half (half milk, half cream)
¾ teaspoon salt
⅛ teaspoon pepper
¼ cup butter or margarine, melted
1 cup shredded Swiss cheese (about ¼ pound)
⅓ cup fine corn flake crumbs

Beat eggs well. Add milk or half and half, salt, pepper and 2 tablespoons melted butter or margarine; mix well. Pour into fry pan. Cook over very low heat, stirring until the mixture starts to set. Spoon into buttered 9-inch pie plate. Sprinkle cheese over top. Combine crumbs and remaining butter or margarine; mix well and sprinkle over cheese. Bake in hot oven (400°F.) about 10 minutes or until golden brown and eggs set. Cut into wedges. Serve with hot buttered French bread slices. Yield: 4 servings.

Scrambled Eggs, Hungarian Style

6 eggs
2 tablespoons milk
¼ teaspoon salt
6 slices bacon, diced
1 cup thinly sliced red onion
½ teaspoon Hungarian sweet red paprika

Combine eggs, milk and salt; beat slightly. Fry bacon until crisp; transfer bacon pieces to paper toweling to drain. Save 2 tablespoons drippings. Cook onion in drippings until tender. Add egg mixture and cook until desired doneness, stirring gently. Fold in bacon pieces; sprinkle with paprika. Yield: 4 servings.

Eggs à la Goldenrod

8 hard-cooked eggs
1 recipe Cream Sauce (page 66)
12 slices hot buttered toast

Cut eggs in half lengthwise; remove yolks and coarsely chop whites. Fold egg whites into hot sauce. Sieve egg yolks. Arrange 6 slices of toast on 6 warm plates. Spoon an equal amount of sauce over toast; sprinkle with sieved egg yolk. Serve with remaining toast slices, cut in half diagonally. Yield: 6 servings.

Lox and Eggs Elegante

1/3 cup butter or margarine
2 cups sliced fresh mushrooms
3/4 cup coarsely chopped Bermuda onion
1 small green pepper, cleaned and chopped
1/2 pound lox (smoked salmon), finely diced
8 eggs, beaten slightly
1/4 cup half and half (half milk, half cream) or
    whipping cream
1 tablespoon chopped parsley
3/4 teaspoon salt
1/4 teaspoon basil
1/8 teaspoon pepper
Dash of hot pepper sauce

Melt butter or margarine in large heavy fry pan over moderate heat. Add mushrooms, onion and green pepper; cover and cook until mushrooms are almost tender, stirring often. Add lox or smoked salmon and cook slightly. Combine eggs, half and half or cream, parsley, salt, basil, pepper and hot pepper sauce; mix. Add egg mixture to fry pan. Mix carefully and cook over low heat, stirring constantly, until eggs are firmness desired. Yield: 6 servings.

Eggs Ranchero

1/2 pound bacon, cut in 1-inch pieces
3/4 cup tomato sauce
1 large tomato, washed, stemmed and coarsely chopped
1/4 cup water
3 green onions, thinly sliced
2 tablespoons finely chopped green pepper
1 clove garlic, minced
1/2 teaspoon chili powder
1 teaspoon salt
8 eggs
1/4 cup milk or half and half (half milk, half cream)
Buttered toast or tortillas, as desired

Cook bacon until crisp; drain bacon pieces on paper toweling and save 3 tablespoons drippings. Keep bacon warm. Prepare sauce. Combine next 7 ingredients and 1/2 teaspoon salt in saucepan. Simmer gently to blend flavors, about 8 to 10 minutes. Combine eggs, milk or half and half and remaining 1/2 teaspoon salt; beat slightly. Heat bacon drippings in fry pan. Add egg mixture; cook over moderate heat stirring gently during cooking. If desired, pile on hot buttered toast or tortillas; top with sauce and hot bacon pieces. Yield: 4 to 6 servings.

Eggs Roberto

1/4 cup butter or margarine
4 scallions or green onions, thinly sliced
8 eggs, beaten slightly
1/4 pound grated or shredded Provolone cheese
2 tablespoons grated Parmesan cheese
8 pitted black olives, sliced
3/4 teaspoon salt
1/8 teaspoon black pepper

Melt butter or margarine in heavy fry pan over moderate heat. Add scallions or onions and cook just until limp. Combine eggs, cheeses, olives, salt and pepper; pour into fry pan. Cook over low heat until cheese melts and eggs are cooked to the desired consistency, stirring often. Delicious served with hot garlic or buttered Italian or French bread. Yield: 4 to 6 servings.

Zucchini Frittata

3 tablespoons olive oil
2 tablespoons butter or margarine
6 to 8 small (4-inch) zucchini, peeled and cut into
    1/4-inch slices
8 eggs
1 teaspoon salt
1/4 teaspoon pepper
1/2 cup grated or shredded Parmesan cheese

Heat oil and butter or margarine in heavy fry pan over moderate heat. Add zucchini and cook just until tender. Combine eggs, salt and pepper; beat slightly and pour over zucchini. Cook until just set. Sprinkle cheese over top; place in broiler, 4 inches from heat source, until cheese is soft and lightly browned. Let stand 2 to 3 minutes; cut in wedges and serve. Yield: 4 to 6 servings.

Shrimp and Eggs

4 slices bacon
1/2 cup chopped green pepper
1/2 cup chopped onion
3/4 teaspoon salt
1/4 teaspoon pepper
1/2 pound small cooked, peeled, deveined shrimp
6 eggs
1/4 cup half and half (half milk, half cream) or milk

Cook bacon in heavy fry pan over moderate heat until crisp; drain bacon pieces on absorbent paper and save drippings. Crumble bacon; save. Cook green pepper and onion in bacon drippings until tender. Add salt, pepper and shrimp; mix and heat. Combine eggs, half and half or milk and bacon; heat slightly. Add to shrimp mixture; cook until eggs are firmness desired, stirring occasionally. Yield: 6 servings.

Egg Indian Curry

Egg Indian Curry

See photo at left

½ cup finely chopped onion
¼ cup butter
1 teaspoon salt
¼ cup flour
1½ cups water or broth
½ cup milk
¼ teaspoon pepper
¼ teaspoon celery seed
½ teaspoon ginger
2 teaspoons curry powder
8 hard-cooked eggs
4 servings hot fluffy cooked rice

Cook onion in butter until tender, but not brown. Add salt and flour; stir until bubbly and well blended. Add seasonings, milk and water or broth. Cook, stirring constantly until smooth and thickened. Add more curry to taste, if desired. Place hot rice in serving dish. Cut an "X" on small end of each egg. Pour curry sauce on rice and attractively place eggs in center. Serve immediately. Yield: 4 servings.

Sherry Eggs on Anchovy Toast

12 eggs
½ teaspoon salt
⅛ teaspoon pepper
¼ cup butter or margarine
¼ cup dry sherry
6 slices hot toast or toasted English muffin halves
Anchovy paste

Combine eggs, salt and pepper; beat slightly and set aside. Melt butter or margarine in heavy fry pan over moderate heat. Add eggs and cook slowly to firmness desired; stir in sherry. Pile eggs on hot toast or toasted English muffin halves spread with anchovy paste. Yield: 6 servings.

South American Eggs

8 eggs
1 teaspoon chili powder
½ teaspoon salt
⅛ teaspoon pepper
3 tablespoons butter or margarine
1 jar (5 or 6 ounce) dried beef, torn into bits
   (about ¾ cup)
1 can (1 pound) tomatoes or tomato wedges
¾ cup shredded process American cheese
Buttered toast, waffle squares, toasted English muffins
   or tortillas

Combine eggs, chili powder, salt and pepper; beat slightly. Set aside. Melt butter or margarine in heavy fry pan over moderate heat. Add dried beef, tomatoes and cheese. Heat slowly until mixture is hot and bubbly, stirring constantly. Stir in egg mixture and cook until mixture thickens, stirring carefully. Serve on hot buttered toast, atop crisp waffle squares, toasted English muffins or tortillas. Yield: 4 to 6 servings.

Eggs Tortino

6 hard-cooked eggs
1 can (2¼ ounce) deviled ham
¼ cup dairy sour cream
2 teaspoons prepared mustard
1 teaspoon horseradish
1 can (1 pound) tomato wedges
1 clove garlic, minced
2 tablespoons chopped parsley
⅓ cup sliced stuffed olives
½ teaspoon oregano
½ teaspoon sugar
1 cup croutons
¼ cup grated Parmesan cheese

Cut eggs in half lengthwise. Remove yolks from whites and mash. Add ham, sour cream, mustard and horseradish; mix well. Fill egg whites with egg yolk mixture. Prepare sauce. Combine tomatoes, garlic, parsley, olives, oregano and sugar in saucepan. Simmer gently 15 minutes to blend flavors. Spoon an equal amount of croutons into bottom of six 6-ounce custard cups or ramekins. Press 2 stuffed egg halves together. Place an egg on croutons in each dish. Spoon an equal amount of sauce over each egg. Sprinkle with Parmesan cheese. Bake in moderate oven (375°F.) about 15 minutes or until heated. Yield: 6 servings.

Deviled Eggs in Mushroom Sauce

12 hard-cooked eggs, cut in half lengthwise
2 teaspoons grated onion
2 teaspoons Worcestershire sauce
1 teaspoon dry mustard
¼ teaspoon pepper
¼ cup salad dressing or mayonnaise
1 tablespoon wine or cider vinegar
2 teaspoons salt
¼ cup butter or margarine
½ pound fresh mushrooms, sliced
¼ cup thinly sliced green onion
3 tablespoons flour
2 cups milk or half and half (half milk, half cream)
   as desired

Remove yolks; save egg whites. Sieve yolks and blend with next 6 ingredients and 1 teaspoon salt. Fill egg whites with mixture, using spoon or a decorator tube in pastry bag, as desired. Melt butter or margarine in heavy fry pan over moderate heat. Add mushrooms and green onion; cook until mushrooms are limp. Sprinkle flour and remaining 1 teaspoon salt over mushrooms; mix well. Add milk or half and half and cook, stirring constantly, until mixture thickens. Arrange 4 egg halves each in 6 buttered individual (6 or 8 ounce) casseroles; pour an equal amount of sauce over eggs. Bake in moderate oven (350°F.) 15 to 20 minutes or until hot and bubbly. Yield: 6 servings.

Eggs Florentine

Eggs Florentine

In Mornay Sauce. See photo at left

⅓ cup butter or margarine
¼ cup flour
¾ teaspoon salt
Dash of cayenne
2 cups milk or half and half (half milk, half cream)
2 packages (10 ounce each) frozen chopped spinach, cooked and drained well
6 poached eggs (page 7)
⅓ cup grated Parmesan cheese
¼ cup heavy cream, whipped, optional

Melt butter or margarine in heavy saucepan over low heat; stir in flour and seasonings. Gradually add milk or half and half; cook, stirring constantly, until smooth and thickened. Set aside. Spread an equal amount of spinach over bottoms of 6 individual baking dishes or one shallow 1½-quart baking dish. Center a depression in spinach in individual casserole or 6 depressions in baking dish. Place a poached egg in each depression. Fold cheese and whipped cream, if desired, into sauce. Pour sauce over eggs. Heat in broiler 3 to 4 inches from heat source until lightly browned and bubbly. Yield: 6 servings.

Eggs à la Rhine

1 cup hot water
2 chicken bouillon cubes
1 chicken breast
Half and half (half milk, half cream)
3 tablespoons butter or margarine
2 tablespoons flour
½ teaspoon salt
Dash of pepper
2 egg yolks, beaten
1 can (4 ounce) sliced mushrooms, drained
2 tablespoons lemon juice
6 poached eggs (page 7)
3 tablespoons chopped parsley

Pour hot water into saucepan. Add bouillon cubes and dissolve. Add chicken breast; cover and cook until tender, 30 to 40 minutes. Cool breast in stock. Remove chicken from bones and cut into julienne strips. Pour stock into measuring cup; add half and half as needed to make 1¼ cups liquid. Melt butter or margarine in heavy saucepan over moderate heat; stir in flour, salt and pepper; add reserved liquid. Cook until slightly thickened stirring constantly. Stir a small amount of sauce into egg yolks then stir egg yolk mixture into remaining sauce. Add mushrooms, chicken strips and lemon juice. Heat slowly, stirring carefully. Pour ½ of sauce into heated serving dish. Arrange poached eggs on sauce; spoon remaining sauce over eggs. Garnish with chopped parsley. Serve on toast points or toasted English muffin halves. Yield: 6 servings.

Deviled Shrimp and Eggs

¼ cup butter or margarine
2 tablespoons chopped onion
¼ cup flour
½ teaspoon salt
½ teaspoon dry mustard
¼ teaspoon paprika
Dash cayenne
2½ cups milk
6 hard-cooked eggs, sliced
1 can (4½ ounce) shrimp, drained
2 tablespoons chopped pimiento
6 heated toast baskets, patty shells or toast points
Lemon wedges or slices, optional

Melt butter or margarine in saucepan. Add onion; cook until soft. Stir in flour and seasonings. Add milk gradually. Cook until thickened, stirring constantly. Fold in eggs, shrimp and pimiento. Heat. Serve in toast baskets or patty shells or on toast points. Garnish with lemon wedges or slices, if desired. Yield: 6 servings.

CURRIED SHRIMP AND EGGS: Follow recipe for Deviled Shrimp and Eggs. Add 1½ teaspoons curry powder with the flour.

Shirred Eggs Gruyere

2 tablespoons butter or margarine, melted
4 slices (⅛-inch) Gruyere cheese
4 eggs
¼ teaspoon salt
Dash of pepper
¾ cup canned tomato sauce
¾ cup shredded Gruyere cheese

Pour an equal amount of butter or margarine in 4 individual shirred egg dishes (or flat ramekins, see page 6). Place a cheese slice in bottom of each dish. Break eggs one at a time into small dish; slip an egg onto each cheese slice. Sprinkle eggs with salt and pepper. Spoon 3 tablespoons tomato sauce around each egg and spinkle 3 tablespoons cheese over top. Bake in moderate oven (375°F.) 10 to 15 minutes or until eggs are firmness desired. Yield: 4 servings.

Shirred Eggs in Cheese Sauce

1 cup shredded process American or Cheddar cheese
1 teaspoon prepared mustard
1 recipe Cream Sauce (page 66)
6 eggs
¼ teaspoon salt
Dash of pepper
Paprika

Add cheese and mustard to cream sauce; stir until cheese is melted. Pour ½ of the sauce into buttered shallow 1½-quart baking dish. Break each egg into a small dish and then carefully slip into sauce in baking dish. Sprinkle salt and pepper over eggs. Spoon remaining sauce over eggs. Sprinkle top with paprika. Bake in slow oven (325°F.) 20 to 25 minutes or until eggs are desired firmness. Yield: 6 servings.

Eggs Divan

6 hard-cooked eggs, cut in half lengthwise
1 can (2¼ ounce) deviled ham
¼ cup salad dressing or mayonnaise
2 teaspoons prepared mustard
2 packages (10 ounce) frozen asparagus
  spears or broccoli, cooked and well-drained
1 teaspoon instant minced onion
½ cup shredded Cheddar or process American cheese
1 recipe Cream Sauce (page 66)

Remove yolks; save egg whites. Mash yolks until free of lumps. Add deviled ham, salad dressing or mayonnaise and mustard; mix well. Fill each white with yolk mixture. Arrange asparagus spears or broccoli in shallow ovenproof platter or casserole. Arrange deviled eggs on asparagus. Stir onion and cheese into cream sauce; stir until cheese melts. Pour over eggs. Place in hot oven (400°F.) 15 to 20 minutes or until hot and bubbly. Yield: 6 servings.

Eggs Bercy

½ pound chicken livers
3 tablespoons butter or margarine
¼ cup finely chopped onion
¼ teaspoon marjoram
¼ teaspoon chervil
½ teaspoon salt
¼ teaspoon pepper
6 eggs

Wash chicken livers. Remove any skin connective tissue; dry on paper towel. Melt 1½ tablespoons butter or margarine in fry pan. Add livers and onion; cook slowly until about ½ done. Chop livers; stir in marjoram, chervil, ¼ teaspoon salt and pepper. Melt remaining butter or margarine; spread over bottom of 1½-quart shallow baking dish. Spread liver mixture evenly over bottom of dish. Break eggs one at a time and turn onto livers. Sprinkle remaining ¼ teaspoon salt over top. Place in slow oven (300°F.) 12 to 15 minutes or until livers finish cooking and eggs are cooked to desired firmness. Yield: 6 servings.

Shaker Eggs

6 hard-cooked eggs, cut in half lengthwise
3 tablespoons salad dressing or mayonnaise
1 teaspoon vinegar
1 teaspoon prepared mustard
½ teaspoon salt
Dash of pepper
1 egg, beaten slightly
½ cup fine cracker or corn flake crumbs
3 tablespoons shortening or cooking oil

Remove yolks from whites of hard-cooked eggs; save egg whites. Mash egg yolks; stir in salad dressing or mayonnaise, vinegar, mustard, salt and pepper; mix well. Fill cavities in egg whites with mixture. Stir any leftover egg yolk mixture into beaten egg. Dip stuffed eggs into egg mixture; drain and roll in crumbs. Heat shortening or cooking oil in heavy fry pan over moderate heat. Brown eggs in hot shortening or oil, turning as needed to brown lightly on all sides (see figure 6 page 6). Serve hot. Yield: 6 servings.

Bacon Cheese Strata

12 slices day old bread
4 eggs, beaten slightly
2½ cups milk
¼ teaspoon dry mustard
1 teaspoon salt
2 teaspoons Worcestershire sauce
½ teaspoon onion salt, optional
Dash of pepper
12 slices process American cheese (12 ounces)
½ cup crisp bacon bits
6 bacon slices, cut in half

Trim crusts from bread slices; arrange ½ of the bread slices over bottom of buttered shallow 2-quart baking dish. Combine eggs, milk and seasonings; beat slightly. Cover bread slices with milk mixture; top each with a cheese slice and sprinkle bacon bits over all. Cover with remaining bread slices. Pour remaining milk mixture over bread. Bake in slow oven (325°F.) about 1 hour, or until set. Fry bacon slices until lightly brown, about ¾ done. Five minutes before end of baking time, top each bread slice with a cheese slice and 2 bacon strips. Return to oven to melt cheese and heat bacon. Cool 10 minutes before serving. Yield: 6 servings.

Eggs Fu Yung

¼ cup butter or margarine
½ cup chopped onion
½ cup diced celery
2 tablespoons diced green pepper
1 can (1 pound) bean sprouts
1 can (6 ounce) water chestnuts, drained and chopped
1 cup chopped cooked chicken, duck, turkey, shrimp,
  crabmeat or pork
6 eggs
1¼ teaspoons salt
2 tablespoons flour
1 tablespoon cornstarch
1 teaspoon sugar
Water
2 tablespoons soy sauce

Melt butter or margarine in heavy fry pan. Add onion, celery and green pepper and cook slowly until tender but not brown. Drain bean sprouts, save liquid. Add bean sprouts, water chestnuts and cooked poultry, seafood or meat to onion mixture. Combine eggs, 1 teaspoon salt and flour; beat until well mixed. Add vegetable mixture; mix well. For each cake pour ¼ cup mixture into a hot lightly oiled fry pan. Spread into a 4-inch cake. Brown on first side; turn carefully and brown second side. Prepare sauce. Combine cornstarch, sugar and remaining ¼ teaspoon salt in small heavy saucepan. Add water as needed to bean sprout liquid to make 1 cup. Add liquid and soy sauce to cornstarch mixture; mix well. Cook, stirring constantly until sauce is thickened and clear. Serve over Eggs Fu Yung cakes. Yield: About 16 cakes, 6 to 8 servings.

Eggs in Curry Sauce

⅓ cup butter or margarine
¾ cup chopped celery
¼ cup chopped green pepper
⅓ cup flour
1½ teaspoons salt
¾ to 1 teaspoon curry powder, or to taste
3 cups half and half (half milk, half cream) or milk
6 hard-cooked eggs, sliced
2 tablespoons chopped well-drained chutney, optional
2 tablespoons chopped pimiento
8 to 12 toasted buttered English muffin halves or
   toast slices

Melt butter or margarine in heavy saucepan over low heat. Add celery and green pepper; cook until tender, not brown. Stir in flour, salt and curry powder. Add half and half or milk; cook until thickened, stirring constantly. Fold in eggs, chutney and pimiento; heat. Serve on 4 to 6 toasted English muffin halves or toast slices. Serve with remaining muffin halves or toast. Yield: 4 to 6 servings.

Egg And Asparagus Casserole

1 package (4½ ounce) potato chips, coarsely
   crushed (2 cups)
1 package (10 ounce) frozen asparagus spears,
   cooked and drained
6 hard-cooked eggs, sliced
1 cup shredded Cheddar or process American cheese
1 recipe Cream Sauce (page 66)

Sprinkle ½ of crushed potato chips over bottom of buttered shallow 1½-quart baking dish. Cover with layers using ½ of asparagus spears, ½ of sliced eggs and ½ of cheese. Repeat layers. Spoon sauce over all; sprinkle with remaining crushed potato chips. Bake in moderate oven (350°F.) 25 to 30 minutes, or until hot and bubbly. Yield: 4 to 6 servings.

Scalloped Eggs and Shrimp

⅓ cup butter or margarine
¼ cup flour
¾ teaspoon salt
¼ teaspoon dry mustard
Dash of pepper
2 cups half and half (half milk, half cream) or milk
1 teaspoon chopped parsley
8 hard-cooked eggs, coarsely chopped
1 cup cooked, peeled, deveined shrimp or 1 can
   (4½ ounce) shrimp, drained
⅓ cup fine bread or cereal crumbs
¼ cup shredded Cheddar or process American cheese

Melt ¼ cup butter or margarine in heavy saucepan over moderate heat. Stir in flour, salt, mustard and pepper. Add half and half or milk and cook until thickened and smooth, stirring constantly. Fold in parsley, eggs and shrimp. Pour into well-buttered shallow 1½-quart casserole. Melt remaining butter or margarine; add crumbs and mix well. Stir in cheese and sprinkle over top of casserole. Bake in moderate oven (350°F.) 25 to 30 minutes or until hot and bubbly. Yield: 4 to 6 servings.

Creamy Egg Chowder

6 slices bacon, diced
2 tablespoons butter or margarine
1 cup sliced onion
⅓ cup diced green pepper
2 tablespoons flour
1 teaspoon salt
¼ teaspoon pepper
2 cups milk
1 cup half and half (half milk, half cream)
1 cup shredded Cheddar cheese
4 hard-cooked eggs, sliced or coarsely chopped
½ teaspoon leaf thyme, optional

Fry bacon until crisp. Drain on paper toweling; pour 2 tablespoons bacon drippings into saucepan. Add butter or margarine and heat. Add onion and cook until limp. Add green pepper. Stir in flour, salt and pepper. Add milk and half and half; cook stirring constantly until thickened. Add cheese; stir until melted. Add eggs and thyme, if used; heat to serving temperature. Pour into bowls; sprinkle with crisp bacon. Yield: About 5 cups chowder, 4 to 6 servings.

Cheese Onion Pie

4 cups thinly sliced onion rings
1 tablespoon butter or margarine
2 cups shredded process American or Cheddar
   cheese (½ pound)
9-inch unbaked pastry shell with high fluted rim
4 medium size eggs
⅔ cup undiluted evaporated milk or half and half
   (half milk, half cream)
1½ teaspoons salt
⅛ teaspoon pepper

Cook onion rings in butter or margarine in heavy fry pan over moderate heat until soft and limp. Spread alternate layers of onion rings and shredded cheese in pastry shell. Combine remaining ingredients in bowl; beat slightly. Place pie on oven rack. Pour egg mixture over onions. Bake in hot oven (400°F.) 30 minutes or until egg mixture "sets." Remove from oven, cool 5 to 10 minutes before serving. Yield: One 9-inch pie, 6 servings.

Swiss Custard Pie

½ pound sliced Swiss cheese, cut in ¼-inch strips
9-inch unbaked pastry shell
5 eggs
1 tablespoon flour
¾ teaspoon salt
¼ teaspoon dry mustard
Dash of pepper
1 cup milk
1 cup half and half (half milk, half cream)
2 tablespoons butter or margarine, melted
3 tomato slices, optional

Arrange cheese strips over bottom of pastry shell. Combine remaining ingredients except tomato slices; beat just until well mixed. Pour into shell. Bake in moderate oven (375°F.) 30 to 35 minutes or until pie is golden brown puffy· filling is set and shell baked. Garnish with half tomato slices, if desired. Yield: One 9-inch pie, 5 to 6 servings.

Salmon Pie

1 can (1 pound) salmon
Milk
3 eggs
1 cup soft bread crumbs
3 tablespoons butter or margarine
1¼ cups diced celery
⅓ cup chopped onion
1½ tablespoons chopped parsley
1½ tablespoons lemon juice
1 teaspoon salt
9-inch unbaked pastry shell

Drain salmon liquid into measuring cup; add milk as needed to make 1 cup liquid. Bone, skin and flake salmon. Combine eggs and liquids; beat slightly. Add bread crumbs; mix and let stand while preparing vegetables. Melt butter or margarine in heavy fry pan over moderate heat. Add celery and onion; cook until celery is tender. Add vegetables, salmon, parsley, lemon juice and salt to egg mixture; mix carefully. Pour into pastry shell. Bake in hot oven (400°F.) 25 to 30 minutes or until filling is set. Let stand 5 to 10 minutes before cutting. Yield: One 9-inch pie, 6 servings.

TUNA PIE: Follow recipe for Salmon Pie and substitute 2 cans (7 ounces each) tuna, drained and flaked, for salmon.

Eggs Poached in Sour Cream Sauce

2 tablespoons butter or margarine
1½ cups dairy sour cream
¼ cup chili sauce or catsup
¼ teaspoon thyme
¾ teaspoon salt
Dash of pepper
6 eggs

Melt butter or margarine in heavy 10-inch fry pan over low heat. Stir in next 5 ingredients. Cover and heat. Break one egg at a time into small dish and slip into hot mixture. Cover and cook over low heat until eggs are desired doneness. Serve on toast. Yield: 6 servings.

Poached Eggs in Red Wine

3 tablespoons butter or margarine
⅔ cup chopped onion
¼ cup chopped celery
1 sliver garlic
2 teaspoons flour
½ teaspoon salt
Dash of pepper
Pinch of thyme
2 cups dry red wine
8 eggs
8 slices buttered toast or toasted English muffin halves

Melt butter or margarine in large heavy fry pan over moderate heat. Add onion, celery and garlic. Cook slowly until onion and celery are tender, not brown. Stir in flour, salt, pepper and thyme. Add wine; mix well. Simmer gently 8 to 10 minutes. Carefully turn each egg into simmering sauce; cover and cook very slowly until egg whites are cooked. Transfer eggs to slices of buttered toast or English muffin halves. Serve with sauce, if desired. Yield: 4 servings.

Eggs Benedict

See photo at right

3 English muffins, split, toasted and buttered
6 slices grilled Canadian bacon or boned rolled fully-cooked ham
6 poached eggs (page 7)
1 recipe Hollandaise Sauce (page 66)

Arrange a hot toasted muffin half on each heated serving plate; top with a slice of Canadian bacon or ham. Center a poached egg on each meat slice; spoon Hollandaise Sauce over egg. Serve at once. Yield: 6 servings.

VARIATIONS: Follow recipe for Eggs Benedict and change as follows:

EGGS BENEDICT PLUS: Top each meat slice with broiled ¼-inch tomato slice before adding egg.

EGGS BENEDICT SUPREME: Top each meat slice with 3 or 4 hot seasoned cooked fresh, frozen or canned asparagus spears before adding egg.

Baked Eggs with Cheese and Canadian Bacon

6 slices (⅜-inch) Canadian bacon
6 eggs
¼ teaspoon salt
Dash of pepper
1 cup shredded process American or Cheddar cheese (¼ pound)
6 buttered toasted English muffin halves

Spread Canadian bacon slices over bottom of buttered shallow 2-quart baking dish. Break an egg onto each meat slice. Sprinkle with salt, pepper and cheese. Bake in moderate oven (350°F.) 10 to 15 minutes or until eggs are cooked to desired doneness. Serve on toasted English muffin halves. Yield: 6 servings.

Eggs in Sour Cream

1 cup (½ pint) dairy sour cream
1 tablespoon milk
1 teaspoon salt
⅛ teaspoon pepper
6 eggs
1 tablespoon butter or margarine, melted
1 teaspoon chopped parsley
4 anchovy fillets, chopped
½ to 1 teaspoon finely chopped chives
¼ cup buttered fine bread crumbs

Combine sour cream, milk, ½ teaspoon salt and pepper; mix. Spread mixture over bottom of well-buttered shallow 1½-quart baking dish. Make 6 wells in sour cream to hold eggs. Break one egg at a time into a small dish. Slide an egg into each well. Drizzle butter or margarine over eggs. Sprinkle remaining ½ teaspoon salt, parsley, anchovies, chives and bread crumbs over top. Bake in moderate oven (350°F.) 10 to 18 minutes or until eggs are desired firmness. Yield: 6 servings.

Eggs Benedict ▶

OMELETS

To Make Plain or French Omelets

Select one of the tested recipes that follow. Assemble equipment (Fig. 1) and mix ingredients. Heat pan over moderately high heat or as recipe suggests. Pan should be hot enough to sizzle and foam butter without turning it brown. Use ½ tablespoon butter for cooking a 2 or 3 egg omelet, 1 tablespoon butter for 6 or 8 egg omelet. Rotate pan (Fig. 2) so butter will coat surface evenly. Pour egg mixture (Fig. 3) into pan; slide pan back and forth slowly over heating unit constantly during cooking. Stir eggs around outside edge of pan with a spatula or a 3 or 4-tined fork (Fig. 4) for about 30 seconds.

Cook eggs until they lose their gloss; let stand 1 or 2 minutes to brown on underside. If a filled omelet is desired the filling should be added at this time.

Omelets

Omelets, plain or puffy, are impressive, delicious, economical, quick and easy to make. There are two basic omelets, the plain or French one and the puffy one with a soufflé-like texture. The difference between the two is determined by the method of mixing and cooking.

The egg yolks and whites for French omelets are beaten together and the omelet cooked over direct heat. When making puffy omelets the yolks and whites are beaten separately, cooked over direct heat until browned on underside, then baked until set.

Plain or French Omelets . . . A Few Tricks Assure Success!

Select the right pan—A heavy aluminum, iron or copper omelet pan with gently sloping sides and about 2 inches deep.

Omelets are tender and moist and cook quicker in the right size pan. Use a 6 or 7-inch pan for 2 or 3 egg omelets, a 10-inch pan for 6 or 8 egg omelets.

Should omelet pans be seasoned?—If the pan is treated with a non-stick surface it should be seasoned, used and cleaned as the manufacturer directs. All other pans should be seasoned as follows before using. It is a good idea to season non-stick surfaces before using the first time.

Season untreated pans this way—Scour surface (not silvered or tinned) with fine steel wool, rinse and dry. Fill with cooking oil to within ¾-inch of top. Heat slowly until fine thread-like lines seem to form in oil and move about in bottom of pan. Turn heat off; cool thoroughly. Save oil for reuse. Wipe pan clean with paper towel. If possible save pan for making omelets only!

To clean pans after use—Don't wash. Wipe surface clean with paper towel. If necessary add salt and rub briskly with paper towel. If washing is necessary pan should be seasoned again before using.

Figure 1   Figure 2

Figure 3   Figure 4

To Roll or Fold Plain or French Omelets

Slide tip of small spatula around outside edge of omelet; rotate pan (Fig. 5) to make sure omelet slides in pan. If there is sticking in spots free omelet with spatula and slip a little butter in so omelet will slide freely. Tip front edge of pan up (Fig. 6A); let omelet slide towards handle then quickly lift handle up (Fig. 6B). With a little push here and there with the tip of a spatula the omelet will roll over and over and out of pan (Fig. 6C) onto hot serving plate.

If a folded omelet is preferred crease it in center and fold or roll in half as directed above; slide onto heated serving dish.

Puffy Omelets or Omelette Soufflé ...
A Few Tricks Assure Success!

Select the right pan—A heavy aluminum, iron or copper omelet pan with gently sloping sides and about 2 inches deep.

These omelets are fluffy and dry and much thicker than the Plain or French Omelet. As the egg whites are beaten separately and folded into the other ingredients these omelets require larger pans. Use a 10-inch pan for a 6 egg omelet.

Because these omelets are finished by baking in the oven it is necessary that the pan selected have an ovenproof handle.

For seasoning and cleaning pans—Refer to page 54.

Figure 5

Figure 6

Figure 7   Figure 8

Figure 9   Figure 10

Figure 11   Figure 12

Figure 13   Figure 14

To Make Puffy Omelet or Omelette Soufflé

Select one of the tested recipes that follow. Assemble equipment (Fig. 7) and mix ingredients (Fig. 8). Heat pan over very very low heat and melt butter or margarine (Fig. 2). Beat egg whites until they hold stiff peaks (Fig. 9). Fold egg yolk mixture into egg whites (Fig. 10). Pour into pan and spread evenly (Fig. 11). Cook over low heat until puffed and lightly browned on bottom (Fig. 12). Bake in moderate oven (350°F.) as instructed by recipe. Remove from oven and cut part way through center (Fig. 13). Fold omelet in half and transfer to a warm plate (Fig. 14).

Plain Omelet

8 eggs
3 tablespoons milk or half and half (half milk,
  half cream)
1¼ teaspoons salt
Dash of pepper
2 tablespoons butter or margarine

Combine eggs, milk or half and half, salt and pepper; beat slightly. Melt butter or margarine in heavy 10-inch fry pan with sloping sides or omelet pan over direct moderate heat. Add egg mixture. Cook over very low heat until set but top is still shiny. To speed cooking run a spatula around edge of pan during cooking; lift omelet and let egg mixture flow below omelet. Fold omelet in half (Fig. 6 page 55). Turn or roll out of pan onto warm platter. Serve at once. Yield: 4 servings.

VARIATIONS: Follow recipe for Plain Omelet and change as follows.

BACON, HAM OR SAUSAGE OMELET: Before folding omelet spread ½ to ¾ cup crisp cooked bacon bits or hot diced fully-cooked ham or sausage over ½ of omelet. Yield: 4 servings.

BLUEBERRY AND SOUR CREAM OMELET: Sprinkle 2 teaspoons confectioners' sugar over 1 cup washed fresh blueberries; mix carefully. Before folding, spread ¼ cup dairy sour cream over ½ of omelet; spoon ½ of berries over cream. Fold omelet and sprinkle surface lightly with additional confectioners' sugar. Serve with remaining berries. Yield: 4 servings.

CHEESE OMELET: Before folding omelet sprinkle ¾ cup shredded Cheddar or American cheese and 2 teaspoons chopped chives over ½ of omelet. Yield: 4 servings.

CHICKEN LIVER OMELET: Sauté 8 to 10 chicken livers in 2 tablespoons butter or margarine until centers are grey in color. Transfer livers to cutting board; remove pan from heat. Cut livers in thin slices or chop; return to pan. Add 1 can (3 ounce) sliced mushrooms, well-drained, 1 tablespoon chopped parsley and ½ teaspoon salt to fry pan. Heat, stirring constantly. Before folding, spread liver mixture over ½ of omelet. Yield: 4 servings.

FANCY STRAWBERRY OMELET: Omit pepper, ½ of the salt and add 1 tablespoon sugar to egg mixture before cooking. Before folding, spoon ⅓ cup thick strawberry jam over ½ of omelet; fold and dust top with confectioners' sugar. Yield: 4 servings.

FLAMING CITRUS OMELET: *(See photo page 59)* Prepare as directed for Fancy Strawberry Omelet (this page) and substitute thick orange marmalade for strawberry jam; pour ¼ cup warmed Cointreau over omelet and ignite. Serve when flame dies. Yield: 4 servings.

FLAMING RUM OMELET: Omit pepper and ½ of the salt and add 1 tablespoon sugar to egg mixture before cooking. Fold omelet, sprinkle with confectioners' sugar. Drizzle ½ cup rum over omelet. Ignite. Serve when flame dies. Yield: 4 servings.

FRUIT OMELET: Omit pepper and ½ teaspoon salt and add 1 tablespoon sugar to egg mixture before cooking. Spread ¾ cup drained canned crushed pineapple, sliced peaches or apricots over ½ of the omelet. Fold and sprinkle top with confectioners' sugar. Yield: 4 servings.

JELLY OMELET: Before folding omelet, spread ½ cup softened jelly (or preserves) over ½ of the omelet. Yield: 4 servings.

MUSHROOM OMELET: Before folding omelet, sprinkle 1 cup sautéed sliced mushrooms over ½ of the omelet. Yield: 4 servings.

HAM AND OLIVE OMELET: Sauté 2 small peeled, seeded and chopped tomatoes in 2 tablespoons butter or margarine; add ½ cup diced fully-cooked ham and 3 tablespoons sliced stuffed olives; heat, stirring often. Before folding, spoon ½ of mixture over ½ of omelet. Spoon remaining ham mixture around omelet. Yield: 4 servings.

OMELET WITH SHERRY-MUSHROOM SAUCE: Sauté ½ pound fresh mushrooms, thinly sliced, in 2 tablespoons butter or margarine until a golden brown. Add 1 tablespoon dry sherry; simmer gently 2 to 3 minutes. Stir in 2 tablespoons cream or half and half (half milk, half cream). Spoon mixture over ½ of omelet just before folding and serve remaining sauce with omelet. Yield: 4 servings.

SPANISH SAUSAGE PEPPER OMELET: Melt 1½ tablespoons butter or margarine in heavy fry pan over low heat. Add ¼ cup chopped green pepper with ½ cup coarsely chopped fully-cooked chorizo (Spanish spicy sausage) and cook until peppers are limp and sausage hot. Before folding, spoon mixture over ½ of omelet and transfer to serving platter. Yield: 4 servings.

STRAWBERRY AND SOUR CREAM OMELET: Sprinkle 2 teaspoons confectioners' sugar over 1 cup thinly sliced strawberries; mix carefully. Before folding, spread ¼ cup dairy sour cream over ½ of omelet. Spoon ½ of strawberries over cream. Fold and sprinkle surface with additional confectioners' sugar. Serve with remaining berries. Yield: 4 servings.

STRAWBERRY OMELET: Omit pepper, ½ of the salt and add 1 tablespoon sugar to egg mixture before cooking. Before folding omelet spoon 1 cup sliced sweetened strawberries over ½ of the omelet. Fold and sprinkle with confectioners' sugar. Yield: 4 servings.

SHRIMP OMELET: Coarsely chop ½ cup cooked and deveined fresh shrimp or 1 can (4½ ounce), drained. Melt 1 tablespoon butter or margarine in fry pan; add shrimp and heat slowly stirring often. Add ½ cup canned tomato sauce and 2 tablespoons shredded or grated Parmesan cheese, ½ teaspoon salt and a dash or two of hot pepper sauce. Just before folding, spoon ⅓ of sauce over ½ of omelet. Fold and serve remaining sauce with omelet. Yield: 4 servings.

French Omelet for One

2 eggs
2 teaspoons milk or cream
¼ teaspoon salt
Dash of pepper
2 teaspoons butter or margarine

Combine first 4 ingredients; beat lightly with a wisk or fork. Heat a 6 or 7-inch fry pan or omelet pan with sloping sides; add butter or margarine and heat until it sizzles. Add egg mixture to pan and cook over moderate heat. Stir once with a fork. Lift edges of omelet all around and let uncooked egg run under omelet. When brown on underside and firm but moist, loosen edges of omelet; shake pan to loosen omelet (see Fig. 5 page 55). Tilt pan downward towards you so omelet will slide down side of pan. Fold ⅓ of omelet to center. Tilt pan up in the opposite direction; roll and turn omelet onto a hot plate with help of spatula (see Fig. 6 page 55). Serve at once. Yield: 1 serving.

Puffy Omelet for Two

2 tablespoons butter or margarine
4 large eggs, separated
¼ teaspoon cream of tartar
½ teaspoon salt
¼ cup milk

Melt butter or margarine in heavy 10-inch fry pan with sloping sides or omelet pan with ovenproof handle (See Fig. 7 to 14 page 55). Let stand over very very low heat. Beat egg whites, cream of tartar and ¼ teaspoon salt until egg whites hold stiff peaks. Beat egg yolks, remaining ¼ teaspoon salt and milk until light and lemony. Carefully fold egg yolk mixture into egg whites until no streaks show. Be careful not to overmix. Pour into pan. Cook over low heat 12 to 15 minutes or until omelet puffs and is browned on bottom. Place in moderate oven (350°F.) 8 to 10 minutes or until top will spring back when touched lightly with finger (or, knife point inserted in center of omelet will come out clean when done). Cut across center, tip pan, carefully loosen omelet from pan with spatula. Fold and turn onto hot serving platter. Yield: 2 to 3 servings.

SWEET OMELET: Follow recipe for Puffy Omelet For Two and add 1½ tablespoons granulated sugar to egg yolks before beating. Before folding, spread ½ of omelet with soft butter or margarine, sprinkle generously with confectioners' sugar and grated orange rind. Fold and dust with confectioners' sugar. Yield: 2 servings.

PUFFY HAM OMELET FOR TWO: Follow recipe for Puffy Omelet For Two and make the following changes: Reduce salt to ¼ teaspoon, substitute 1 tablespoon warm water for milk and stir ¼ to ½ cup finely chopped fully-cooked ham into egg yolk mixture before adding to egg whites. Yield: 2 servings.

Puffy Salmon Omelet

2 tablespoons butter or margarine
6 egg whites
¾ teaspoon salt
6 egg yolks
⅓ cup milk or half and half (half milk, half cream)
2 teaspoons chopped parsley
1 teaspoon chopped onion
⅛ teaspoon oregano
⅛ teaspoon pepper
1 can (7¾-ounce) salmon, drained, boned and flaked

Melt butter or margarine in heavy 10-inch fry pan with sloping sides of omelet pan with ovenproof handle over very very low heat. Beat egg whites and salt until they hold soft peaks. Beat egg yolks until thick and lemon colored. Stir in milk or half and half, parsley, onion, oregano, pepper and salmon. Fold egg yolk mixture into egg whites. Pour into fry pan and spread evenly. Cook over low heat for 8 to 10 minutes or until puffed and lightly browned on sides and bottom. Bake in moderate oven (350°F.) 12 to 15 minutes or until knife inserted in center comes out clean. Cut part way through center of omelet; fold in half. Serve at once. Yield: 6 servings.

Fluffy Omelet with Vegetable Cheese Sauce

6 tablespoons butter or margarine
¼ cup flour
2 teaspoons salt
¼ teaspoon onion or seasoned salt
⅛ teaspoon pepper
2 cups milk
1 teaspoon prepared mustard
6 eggs, separated
1 package (10 ounce) frozen mixed vegetables, partially defrosted and broken apart
1 cup shredded process American or Cheddar cheese (¼ pound)

Melt 1 tablespoon butter or margarine in heavy 10-inch fry pan with ovenproof handle. Place over very very low heat. Melt 4 tablespoons butter or margarine; stir in flour, 1 teaspoon salt, onion or seasoned salt and pepper. Add milk and cook, stirring constantly, until smooth and thickened. Stir in mustard. Keep hot. Beat egg yolks until thick and lemon colored; mix in ¾ cup sauce. Beat egg whites and ½ teaspoon salt until they hold soft peaks. Carefully but thoroughly fold in egg yolk mixture. Pour into prepared fry pan; cook over low heat 12 to 15 minutes or until lightly browned on sides and bottom. Bake in moderate oven (350°F.) about 15 minutes or until set. While omelet is baking combine vegetables, remaining 1 tablespoon butter or margarine and ½ teaspoon salt; cover and cook. Stir into remaining sauce; spoon over baked omelet and sprinkle with cheese. Cut in wedges to serve. Yield: 4 servings.

Spanish Dinner Omelet

3 tablespoons butter or margarine
½ cup coarsely chopped onion
¾ cup diced raw potato (about 1 medium)
1 package (10 ounce) frozen cut asparagus, defrosted
   and drained or 1 pound fresh asparagus, washed
   and cut into 1-inch lengths
1 teaspoon salt
½ pound frankfurters or fully-cooked Spanish
   sausage, cut into ¼ inch slices
6 eggs
½ cup milk
1½ teaspoons paprika
⅛ teaspoon pepper

Melt butter or margarine in heavy shallow 12-inch frying or Spanish omelet pan. Add onion, potato and asparagus; sprinkle ½ teaspoon salt over mixture. Cover; cook slowly about 12 minutes or until vegetables are almost tender. Add sausage and heat. Combine eggs, milk, paprika, remaining salt and pepper; beat slightly and pour over vegetables. Cook over very low heat 10 to 12 minutes or until egg mixture is set. Lift edges of omelet with spatula or knife during cooking to allow uncooked egg mixture to flow underneath omelet and cook. Don't fold. To serve, cut in quarters. Yield: 4 servings.

Elegant Omelet

2 slices bacon, diced
3 tablespoons chopped celery
1 tablespoon chopped onion
1 teaspoon minced parsley, optional
½ cup Cream Sauce (page 66)
2 tablespoons dairy sour cream
1 tablespoon white wine, optional
1 teaspoon Worcestershire sauce
½ cup diced or chopped cooked chicken
1 recipe Plain Omelet (page 56)

Cook bacon in heavy fry pan until crisp and lightly browned, stirring often. Transfer bacon to paper toweling to drain. Remove all but 1 tablespoon drippings from pan. Sauté celery and onion in drippings until tender. Add remaining ingredients and bacon; mix and heat. Keep hot in fry pan while preparing omelet. Before folding omelet spread ⅓ of mixture over ½ of omelet; fold and transfer to serving platter. Spoon remaining sauce over top. Yield: 4 servings.

Strawberry Rum Omelet

8 eggs
2 tablespoons milk
½ teaspoon salt
1½ tablespoons sugar
1 tablespoon butter or margarine
½ cup strawberry preserves
¼ cup rum, warmed

Combine eggs, milk, salt and sugar; beat slightly. Melt butter in a 10-inch omelet pan or fry pan with sloping sides. Pour in egg mixture. Cook over low heat, lifting omelet gently with a spatula as it cooks on the bottom, so uncooked mixture will run underneath. When omelet is slightly firm on top, remove from heat; spread ½ of top with strawberry preserves. Fold over other half; place on table top heating unit. Pour hot rum over top; ignite. Serve when flame dies. Yield: 4 servings.

Raspberry Dessert Omelet

2 tablespoons butter or margarine
6 eggs, separated
½ teaspoon salt
¼ teaspoon cream of tartar
2 teaspoons granulated sugar
¼ cup milk
¼ cup thick raspberry preserves
1 tablespoon orange juice
1 teaspoon grated orange rind
1 tablespoon kirsch, optional
1 tablespoon confectioners' sugar

Melt butter or margarine in 10-inch omelet or round fry pan with sloping sides and ovenproof handle. Place over very very low heat. Combine egg whites, salt and cream of tartar; beat until egg whites hold stiff peaks. Add granulated sugar and mix well. Beat egg yolks and milk until thick and lemon colored. Carefully fold egg yolks into egg whites. Brush butter or margarine over bottom and sides of pan. Pour mixture into pan. Cook over medium heat 8 to 10 minutes or until lightly browned on sides and bottom. Place in moderate oven (350°F.) about 15 minutes or until set and golden brown. While omelet is baking combine preserves, orange juice and rind and kirsch, if desired; mix. Loosen edges of omelet with spatula; turn top side down on plate; spread filling over ½ of omelet and fold in half. Sprinkle with confectioners' sugar. Yield: 4 servings.

Flaming Citrus Omelet (page 56) ▶

SALADS

Caesar Salad

½ cup salad oil
1 clove garlic, thinly sliced
2 cups firm bread cubes (½-inch)
3 tablespoons lemon juice
1 teaspoon Worcestershire sauce
1 teaspoon salt
¼ teaspoon dry mustard
⅛ teaspoon pepper
2 eggs
8 cups crisp torn salad greens (romaine, Boston, bibb
   and head lettuce)
⅓ cup shredded Parmesan cheese
1 hard-cooked egg, chopped
6 to 8 anchovy fillets, optional

Combine salad oil and garlic; let stand about 1 hour.
Heat ¼ cup oil and garlic in fry pan until garlic browns;
remove garlic from pan. Add bread cubes; brown on all
sides, stirring as needed to brown evenly. Drain and
cool. Combine remaining ¼ cup oil, lemon juice, Worcestershire sauce, salt, mustard and pepper; mix. Cook
2 eggs in boiling water 1 minute; cool in cold water at
once. Turn salad greens into salad bowl. Break eggs;
beat slightly and add to salad greens; toss to coat
greens well. Add oil mixture; toss. Add bread cubes,
cheese and hard-cooked egg; toss lightly. Top with
anchovy fillets, if desired. Serve at once. Yield: 6 to 8
servings.

Danish Salad

1 pound fresh spinach, washed, drained and torn into
   bite-size pieces
1 can (1 pound) sliced beets, drained (about 1¾ cups)
½ cup thinly sliced onions, separated into rings
½ teaspoon salt
Dash of pepper
4 hard-cooked eggs, cut in wedges
Blue Cheese Dressing (recipe follows)

Combine first 3 ingredients in salad bowl; season with
salt and pepper. Toss lightly. Top with egg wedges;
serve with Blue Cheese Dressing. Yield: 4 to 6 servings.

Blue Cheese Dressing

1 cup salad dressing or mayonnaise
1 cup dairy sour cream
2 teaspoons lemon juice
⅓ to ½ cup crumbled blue or Roquefort cheese

Combine ingredients; mix well. Yield: About 2⅓ cups.

Egg Salad Mold Supreme

See photo at right

Salad:
1 cup cold water
2 envelopes unflavored gelatin
1½ cups mayonnaise
1 teaspoon salt
6 drops hot pepper sauce
1 tablespoon grated onion
2 tablespoons lemon juice
12 hard-cooked eggs, sliced
¼ cup chopped parsley
½ cup chopped celery

Filling:
¼ cup butter or margarine
2 tablespoons flour
½ cup button mushrooms
2 cups cooked chicken, diced
1 cup cooked peas

SALAD: In top of double boiler mix gelatin with cold
water; place over boiling water until gelatin is completely dissolved. Cool slightly. Add mayonnaise, salt,
hot red pepper sauce, lemon juice and grated onion.
Arrange center slices of hard-cooked eggs in bottom
of an oiled 1 to 1½-quart ring mold. Separate remaining yolks and whites of eggs. Chop egg whites and
combine with half of gelatin mixture. Sieve the yolks
and combine with remaining half of gelatin mixture.
Chill until slightly thickened. Pour slightly thickened
yolk mixture into ring mold. Sprinkle celery and parsley
over yolk mixture. Spoon egg white mixture into mold
and chill until firm.

FILLING: Melt butter or margarine in skillet; add flour
and blend. Add mushrooms, peas and chicken; heat
thoroughly. Unmold salad on a serving plate garnished
with parsley or other salad greens and fill center with
chicken mixture. Yield: 8 to 10 servings.

Hot Egg Salad

8 hard-cooked eggs, coarsely chopped
2 cups thinly sliced celery
1 cup salad dressing or mayonnaise
1 tablespoon chopped parsley
¾ teaspoon dry mustard
½ teaspoon salt
¼ teaspoon onion salt
Dash of pepper
1½ tablespoons butter or margarine, melted
⅔ cup wheat germ
⅓ cup coarsely chopped pecans

Combine eggs, celery, salad dressing or mayonnaise,
parsley and seasonings; mix. Spoon into a well-buttered
shallow 1½-quart casserole. Bake in moderate oven
(375°F.) 25 to 30 minutes or until hot. Combine butter
or margarine, wheat germ and pecans; mix well. Sprinkle wheat germ mixture over salad 15 minutes before
end of baking time. Serve hot. Yield: 4 to 6 servings.

Egg Salad Mold Supreme

Pickled Eggs

4 cups cider vinegar
1 cup water
1 tablespoon peppercorns
1 tablespoon whole allspice
1 tablespoon finely chopped ginger root or
   ½ teaspoon ginger
2 teaspoons whole cloves
1 teaspoon salt
½ teaspoon nutmeg or mace
12 hard-cooked eggs, shelled

Combine first 8 ingredients in saucepan. Bring to a boil; simmer gently 10 minutes and strain. Pack eggs in hot sterilized jars; pour hot liquid over eggs. Seal jars. Cool, then store in cool place. Use in 4 to 5 days. Use as salad or appetizer. Yield: 12 eggs.

Salmon Egg Macaroni Salad

¾ cup mayonnaise or salad dressing
1 tablespoon lemon juice
½ teaspoon salt
½ teaspoon curry powder, optional
2 dashes hot red pepper sauce
2 cups drained cooked elbow macaroni, chilled
⅔ cup thinly sliced celery
½ cup diced peeled cucumber
⅓ cup diced sweet pickle
4 hard-cooked eggs, sliced
1 can (1 pound) salmon, drained, boned and flaked
Crisp salad greens

Combine first 5 ingredients; mix well. Add macaroni, celery, cucumber and pickle; mix carefully. Add eggs and salmon; toss lightly. Serve on crisp salad greens. Yield: 6 servings.

Egg and Ham Salad

6 hard-cooked eggs, coarsely chopped
2 cups drained cooked macaroni, chilled
1½ cups diced cooked ham
1 cup sliced celery
¼ cup diced dill pickle
¼ cup sliced stuffed olives
¾ cup salad dressing or mayonnaise
¾ teaspoon salt

Combine ingredients; mix lightly. Chill well, about 1 hour, before serving. Serve on crisp salad greens. Yield: 6 servings.

Picnic Salad

1 package (7 ounce) elbow macaroni, cooked, blanched, drained and cooled
4 hard-cooked eggs, sliced
2 packages (6 or 7 ounce) sliced bologna, salami or favorite cold cuts, or 1 pound fully-cooked frankfurters, coarsely chopped
1½ cups thinly sliced celery
⅓ cup coarsely chopped onions
⅓ cup diced process American or Cheddar cheese
1 cup salad dressing or mayonnaise
¼ cup chili sauce or catsup
1¼ teaspoons salt
⅛ teaspoon pepper
Salad greens

Combine first 6 ingredients in large bowl. Combine next 4 ingredients; mix well. Pour over salad ingredients; mix carefully but well. Serve on salad greens. Yield: 6 to 8 servings.

Oriental Deviled Egg Salad

6 hard-cooked eggs, cut in half lengthwise
¼ cup salad dressing or mayonnaise
4 slices crisp cooked bacon, crumbled into bits
¼ cup finely chopped drained chutney or well-drained sweet pickle relish
2 tablespoons finely chopped celery
1 teaspoon curry powder
¼ teaspoon salt
Pimiento or black olives for garnish
Salad greens

Remove yolks from whites; save whites. Mash yolks. Blend in salad dressing or mayonnaise, bacon bits, chutney or pickle relish, celery, curry powder and salt. Spoon egg yolk mixture into egg whites. Garnish with bits of pimiento or strips of black olive. Arrange on crisp lettuce leaves. Yield: 12 stuffed egg halves, 6 salad servings.

Sour Cream Potato Salad

6 cups sliced chilled cooked potatoes
1 cup diced (½ inch) peeled cucumber
¾ cup sliced radishes
⅔ cup thinly sliced celery
⅓ cup thinly sliced green onions
6 hard-cooked eggs, sliced
1 cup dairy sour cream
¾ cup mayonnaise or salad dressing
2 tablespoons vinegar
2 teaspoons prepared mustard
1½ teaspoons salt
⅛ teaspoon pepper
½ teaspoon celery seed
Salad greens

Combine first 5 ingredients and 4 sliced eggs in large mixing bowl. Combine sour cream, mayonnaise or salad dressing, vinegar, mustard, salt, pepper and celery seed; mix. Add to salad ingredients; mix carefully. Arrange on salad greens; garnish with remaining sliced hard-cooked eggs. Yield: 8 servings.

Novel Shrimp Salad

1 cup cooked deveined fresh or canned shrimp, cut into bite-size pieces
1 can (5 ounce) water chestnuts, drained and sliced
½ cup thinly sliced celery
1½ cups cooled cooked blanched rice
4 hard-cooked eggs, coarsely chopped
¼ cup sliced ripe or stuffed olives
2 teaspoons finely chopped onion
1¼ cups salad dressing or mayonnaise
½ teaspoon salt
½ teaspoon curry powder, optional
Salad greens
¼ cup toasted slivered almonds

Combine first 7 ingredients in bowl; toss lightly. Combine salad dressing or mayonnaise, salt and curry powder; mix. Add dressing to salad ingredients; mix carefully. Spoon onto salad greens and garnish with toasted almonds. Yield: About 6 servings.

SANDWICH SPREADS

Denver Sandwiches with Cheese

3 tablespoons butter or margarine
3 tablespoons finely chopped onion
3 tablespoons finely chopped green pepper
4 eggs, beaten
¼ cup milk
¼ teaspoon salt
Dash of pepper
4 slices process American or Cheddar cheese
8 slices hot buttered toast

Melt butter or margarine in heavy 10-inch fry pan over moderate heat. Add onion and green pepper and cook until tender. While vegetables are cooking combine eggs, milk, salt and pepper. Pour into fry pan; stir to mix. Cover; cook over low heat until eggs "set." Remove cover; loosen eggs from edges of pan with spatula. Place cheese slices on eggs; cover and let cheese soften. Cut into 8 even wedges; arrange on toast slices and serve open-face or closed sandwich style. Yield: 4 servings.

Egg-Salad Rolls

4 hard-cooked eggs, chopped
¼ cup salad dressing or mayonnaise
1 tablespoon French dressing
3 tablespoons chopped stuffed green olives
½ teaspoon salt
½ teaspoon prepared mustard
⅛ teaspoon prepared horseradish
6 lightly buttered frankfurter rolls
6 washed crisp lettuce leaves

Combine first 7 ingredients; mix well. Fill rolls; top with a crisp lettuce leaf and close. Yield: 6 sandwich rolls.

Egg Salad Sandwich Spread

4 hard-cooked eggs, finely chopped
½ cup salad dressing or mayonnaise
½ cup finely chopped celery
3 tablespoons well-drained pickle relish
1 teaspoon prepared mustard
½ teaspoon celery salt
½ teaspoon salt

Combine ingredients; mix well. Chill. Yield: About 2 cups, enough filling for 6 to 8 sandwiches.

BACON 'N EGG SANDWICH SPREAD: Fry or broil 6 to 8 slices bacon until crisp; break into bits. Cool and fold into Egg Salad Sandwich Spread. Yield: About 2¼ cups.

HAM AND EGG SALAD SANDWICH SPREAD: Fold an additional ¼ cup salad dressing or mayonnaise and ½ to ⅔ cup finely chopped cooked ham into Egg Salad Sandwich Spread. Yield: About 2½ cups.

Chicken Salad Spread

4 hard-cooked eggs, finely chopped
1 cup diced cooked chicken
½ cup finely chopped celery
¾ cup salad dressing or mayonnaise
2 tablespoons chopped pimiento
1 tablespoon finely chopped onion
½ teaspoon salt

Combine ingredients; mix well. Chill. Yield: About 3 cups, enough filling for 8 to 10 sandwiches.

CRABMEAT SALAD SPREAD: Follow recipe for Chicken Salad Spread. Substitute 1 package (6 ounce) frozen crabmeat, defrosted and flaked, for the chicken called for. Substitute 1 tablespoon lemon juice for the onion. Yield: About 3 cups.

Egg Salami Spread

1 package (8 ounce) cream cheese, room temperature
1 teaspoon prepared horseradish
2 teaspoons prepared mustard
¼ teaspoon salt
½ cup salad dressing or mayonnaise
4 hard-cooked eggs, finely chopped
1 cup finely chopped hard salami

Combine cream cheese, horseradish, mustard and salt; beat until smooth. Beat in salad dressing or mayonnaise. Stir in eggs and salami. Chill. Yield: About 2½ cups, enough filling for 8 to 10 sandwiches.

Smoky Egg Spread

⅔ cup salad dressing or mayonnaise
2 teaspoons prepared mustard
1 teaspoon Worcestershire sauce
½ teaspoon seasoned salt
6 hard-cooked eggs, finely chopped
4 slices bacon, diced and fried crisp
3 fully-cooked smoked sausage links or hot dogs, finely chopped

Combine salad dressing or mayonnaise, mustard, Worcestershire sauce and salt; mix well. Stir in eggs, bacon and sausage. If desired salad dressing or mayonnaise may be added. Yield: About 2 cups.

Hot Egg-Fish Buns

6 hard-cooked eggs, chopped
1 cup flaked or chopped cooked fish (salmon, tuna or shrimp)
⅔ cup salad dressing or mayonnaise
½ cup well-drained chopped sweet pickle
¼ cup chopped green pepper
2 tablespoons finely chopped onion
½ teaspoon salt
8 hamburger buns, buttered
8 slices (½ pound) process American cheese

Combine ingredients, except buns and cheese; mix well. Spread equal amounts of salad over bottoms of buns. Top each with a cheese slice; cover with bun top. Wrap each bun in aluminum foil. Place on baking sheet in slow oven (325°F.) about 25 minutes or just until heated. Yield: 8 buns.

SAUCES

English Lemon Curd

2 lemons
Water
½ cup butter or margarine
1 cup sugar
⅛ teaspoon salt
3 eggs, beaten

Grate yellow rind from lemons and squeeze lemon juice into measuring cup. Add water as needed to make ½ cup liquid. Melt butter or margarine in top of double boiler or heavy saucepan. Add sugar slowly stirring constantly until well blended. Add lemon juice, water and salt. Cook until sugar is dissolved. Stir 3 tablespoons of butter-sugar mixture into eggs then stir eggs into remaining butter-sugar mixture. Place over low heat; cook until mixture coats the spoon, stirring constantly. Stir in lemon rind. Serve warm or cold. Yield: About 2¼ cups.

Chocolate Custard Sauce

2 egg yolks, beaten
1½ cups sugar
½ teaspoon flour
¼ teaspoon salt
1 square (1 ounce) unsweetened chocolate, melted
1 cup half and half (half milk, half cream) or milk
1¼ teaspoons vanilla

Combine egg yolks, sugar, flour, salt and chocolate. Stir until blended. Add half and half or milk; mix well. Cook in top of double boiler over gently simmering water, stirring constantly, until mixture coats a spoon. Remove from heat; stir in vanilla. Cool. Yield: 1¼ cups.

Cream Sauce

¼ cup butter or margarine
¼ cup flour
½ teaspoon salt
Dash of pepper
2 cups milk or half and half (half milk, half cream)

Melt butter or margarine in heavy saucepan over low heat. Stir in flour and seasonings. Stir in milk or half and half slowly and cook until thick and smooth, stirring constantly. Yield: About 2¼ cups.

CHEESE SAUCE: Prepare Cream Sauce and add 1 to 2 cups shredded process or natural American or Swiss cheese and ½ teaspoon prepared mustard to sauce; stir until cheese is melted. Yield: About 2¾ cups.

CURRY SAUCE: Prepare Cream Sauce and blend 2 to 3 teaspoons curry powder, 1 teaspoon sugar, ⅛ teaspoon ginger and ¼ cup minced onion into butter or margarine. Cook, stirring constantly, until onion is tender before adding flour.

EGG SAUCE: Fold 1 teaspoon prepared mustard, 2 tablespoons diced pimiento and 3 hard-cooked eggs, coarsely chopped into hot Cream Sauce (above). Yield: About 3 cups.

Apricot Puree

1½ cups dried apricots, quartered
¾ cup hot water

Combine apricots and water in saucepan. Bring to a boil; cover and simmer 5 to 6 minutes. Turn heat off and cool with cover on. Whiz drained apricots and ⅓ cup apricot liquid and water, if needed in electric blender until smooth or put through sieve. Yield: About 1 cup puree.

Brandy Sauce

4 egg yolks
⅓ cup sugar
¼ cup brandy
1 cup whipped cream or dessert topping

Combine egg yolks, sugar and brandy in top of double boiler; beat until very thick and fluffy. Cook over gently simmering water stirring constantly until thickened. Chill. Just before serving fold in whipped cream or dessert topping. Yield: 1¾ cups.

Custard Sauce

2 eggs
¼ cup sugar
⅛ teaspoon salt
1⅓ cups milk, scalded
1 teaspoon vanilla
¼ teaspoon nutmeg, optional

Combine eggs, sugar and salt in bowl; beat slightly. Add milk gradually, stirring constantly. Pour into top of double boiler. Cook over simmering water, stirring constantly, until mixture is thick enough to coat the spoon. Pour into bowl; cool quickly, stirring often. Stir in vanilla and nutmeg, if desired. Cover; chill until served. Yield: About 1½ cups sauce.

Hollandaise Sauce

Gourmet
INTERNATIONAL

1 cup butter or margarine
½ teaspoon salt
Dash of cayenne
2 tablespoons lemon juice
1 tablespoon hot water
3 egg yolks

Melt butter or margarine in top of double boiler, stirring constantly until creamy (don't let water touch top part of double boiler). Add salt, cayenne, lemon juice and water, 2 or 3 drops at a time, beating constantly with rotary or electric beater. Remove from heat. Add egg yolks, one at a time, beating constantly during addition and until mixture is light and fluffy. Place over water and cook, stirring constantly, until glossy and slightly thickened. Serve at once. Yield: About 1⅓ cups.

Bearnaise Sauce

Gourmet
INTERNATIONAL

½ cup butter or margarine
¼ cup water or dry white wine
3 tablespoons tarragon or cider vinegar
2 teaspoons finely chopped onions or shallots
¼ teaspoon salt
Dash of pepper
3 egg yolks
½ cup mayonnaise or salad dressing

Combine first 7 ingredients in container of an electric blender, if available. Whiz until ingredients are finely chopped. If no blender is available beat with beater until light and fluffy. Pour into saucepan. Cook over very low heat, stirring constantly until mixture thickens. Remove from heat; stir in mayonnaise or salad dressing. Serve with meat, fish, or seafood fondue dishes or with favorite steaks or burgers. Yield: About 1½ cups.

Cold Chiffon Sauce for Fish

4 hard-cooked eggs, finely chopped
1 tablespoon prepared mustard
½ teaspoon salt
Dash of cayenne or pepper
1 cup mayonnaise or salad dressing
1 small dill pickle, finely chopped or 2 tablespoons
    drained capers
2 pitted black olives, finely chopped

Combine all ingredients in bowl; mix well. Chill. Serve with cold salmon, tuna or other fish. Yield: About 1¼ cups.

SOUFFLÉS

To prepare a soufflé—Assemble equipment and ingredients (Fig. 1) and preheat oven. Prepare sauce and other ingredients such as cheese, meat, fruit, etc.

Beating and handling of egg whites is most important! . . . Use room temperature egg whites; beat whites (Fig. 2) until they hold their shape, are glossy but not dry and then use them quickly before air escapes.

Combine egg whites and sauce base . . . folding gently in a circular motion, down one side of bowl and up through center, turning bowl slightly after each folding (Fig. 3 & 4).

Pour mixture into prepared soufflé dish . . . and if a crown or top hat is desired run the point of a silver knife, ½-inch deep, in a circle about 1½ inches in from edge of dish (Fig. 5).

To get an extra high soufflé use a Collar (Fig. 6). Use clean paper, well buttered, tied around soufflé dish or held in place by rubber bands.

Soufflés

Soufflés are very special foods! Delicious, dramatic and easy to make.

Traditional soufflés are hot glamorous foods made by folding stiffly beaten egg whites into a sauce and adding cheese, fish, fruit, vegetables, chocolate or a fine liqueur for flavor.

Delicious cold feather-light gelatin dishes called soufflés have no relationship to the soufflés made famous by French chefs. These have become quite popular probably because they can be made ahead of serving time.

A Few Simple Soufflé Making Secrets

Select a tested recipe—There's a fine recipe for most every occasion on the following pages. Study the recipe so preparation will be fast and easy.

Use the right tools—Tools are not expensive or hard to find. You'll want a big wire whisk or portable electric mixer, round bottom mixing bowl, wooden spoon or wide rubber spatula and the right size soufflé dish (see recipe).

A wire whisk will whip the greatest amount of air into egg whites with the least effort. A portable electric mixer may be substituted for the whisk since it can be moved about the bowl permitting uniform beating of whites.

Many soufflé dishes can be made more exciting by first preparing the soufflé dish in the following manner:

Grease soufflé dish with shortening or butter and refrigerate. When chilled, spread again with shortening or butter. Sprinkle dish with Parmesan cheese, flour or dried bread crumbs and shake to coat sides and bottom of dish; shake off excess crumbs. When serving try to spoon a portion of the crust with each serving. Especially good with vegetable and cheese soufflés.

Figure 1   Figure 2

Figure 3   Figure 4

Figure 5   Figure 6

Bake . . . on rack in center of preheated oven. Don't open door until 5 minutes before end of baking time.

Soufflé is done . . . when puffed high above top of dish, browned and firm. To test for firmness press tip of finger on top of soufflé or move oven rack back and forth gently to see if top is firm. If top or crown shakes close oven door carefully, bake 5 minutes and check again.

Soufflés will not wait for late-comers . . . serve them at once before they start to fall!

Cheese Soufflé

¼ cup butter or margarine
¼ cup flour
¾ teaspoon salt
⅛ teaspoon pepper
1½ cups milk
2 cups shredded sharp Cheddar or process American
   cheese (½ pound)
6 eggs, separated

Melt butter or margarine; stir in flour, salt and pepper. Add milk, stirring constantly. Cook, stirring constantly, until sauce is smooth and thickened. Remove from heat. Add cheese; stir until melted. Add well-beaten egg yolks slowly stirring briskly. Cool slightly. Beat egg whites until they hold soft peaks. Carefully fold sauce into egg whites. Pour into ungreased 2-quart soufflé dish or casserole. For an attractive "top hat" run tip of knife around casserole 1 inch in from edge (Fig. 5 page 67). Bake in slow oven (300°F.) about 1¼ hours or until top is firm and a golden brown. Serve at once. Yield: 6 servings.

VARIATIONS: Follow recipe for Cheese Soufflé and change as follows.

CHEESE HERB SOUFFLÉ: Add ½ teaspoon fines herbes blend and ¼ teaspoon dry mustard with flour and salt.

BACON SOUFFLÉ: Use bacon drippings instead of butter or margarine, if desired, and fold ½ cup crisp bacon bits into sauce before folding into egg whites.

HAM AND CHEESE SOUFFLÉ: Stir ⅔ cup finely chopped ham into sauce before folding into egg whites.

VEGETABLE SOUFFLÉ: Spread 1 cup well-drained canned or cooked frozen or fresh vegetable over bottom of soufflé dish. Pour soufflé mixture in on top of vegetable.

Seafood Soufflé

⅓ cup finely chopped celery
⅓ cup finely chopped onion
⅓ cup butter or margarine
⅓ cup flour
1 teaspoon salt
1½ cups milk
4 eggs, separated
1 cup flaked cooked lobster meat or crabmeat
1 tablespoon lemon juice
¼ teaspoon cream of tartar

Cook celery and onion in butter or margarine until onion is tender, not brown. Stir in flour and salt. Add milk; cook, stirring constantly until thickened. Beat egg yolks slightly. Stir a small amount of hot mixture into egg yolks, at a time, stirring constantly. Fold in lobster or crabmeat and lemon juice. Combine egg whites and cream of tartar. Beat until egg whites hold soft peaks. Carefully fold into yolk mixture. Pour into ungreased 2-quart soufflé dish or casserole. Bake in moderate oven (350°F.) 45 minutes or until done. Serve at once, plain or with Hollandaise Sauce (page 66). Yield: 6 to 8 servings.

Sky High Cheese Soufflé

See photo at right

½ cup butter or margarine
½ cup flour
1 teaspoon salt
Dash of pepper
2 cups milk
2 cups shredded sharp Cheddar cheese (½ pound)
8 eggs, separated

Melt butter or margarine in heavy saucepan over moderate heat. Stir in flour and seasonings. Add milk and cook over low heat until sauce is thickened and smooth, stirring constantly. Add cheese; stir until it melts. Remove from heat. Beat egg yolks until light; add to sauce slowly in a fine stream, beating constantly. Beat egg whites until they hold stiff peaks. Carefully fold sauce into egg whites. Pour into well-buttered 2½-quart soufflé dish or casserole. For an attractive "top hat" run tip of knife around casserole 1 inch in from edge (see Fig. 5 page 67). Bake in very hot oven (475°F.) 10 minutes. Lower heat to hot oven (400°F.); bake 25 to 30 minutes or until nicely browned, puffed and fairly firm to touch. Serve at once. Yield: 6 servings.

Swiss Cheese Soufflé

⅓ cup butter or margarine
⅓ cup flour
1¼ teaspoons salt
⅛ teaspoon pepper
1½ cups milk
1½ teaspoons Worcestershire sauce
2 cups shredded natural Swiss cheese (½ pound)
6 eggs, separated

Melt butter or margarine in heavy saucepan over moderate heat. Stir in flour, salt and pepper. Stir in milk and cook until thickened and smooth, stirring constantly. Remove from heat; add Worcestershire sauce and cheese and stir until cheese is melted. Beat egg yolks until thick and fluffy; add a small amount of hot sauce; beat well and stir into remaining sauce. Beat egg whites until they hold soft peaks; carefully fold into cheese mixture. Pour into ungreased 2-quart soufflé or casserole. Set in pan of hot water. Bake in moderate oven (350°F.) 50 to 55 minutes or until puffed browned and firm. Serve at once. Yield: 6 servings.

4-Egg Cheese Soufflé

3 tablespoons butter or margarine
¼ cup flour
½ teaspoon salt
Dash of pepper
1 cup milk
2 cups shredded process American or Cheddar
   cheese (½ pound)
4 eggs

Prepare as directed for Cheese Soufflé (this page) except use a 1½ quart soufflé dish or casserole. Serve at once. Yield: 4 servings.

Sky High Cheese Soufflé

Spinach Soufflé

See photo at right

2½ cups drained cooked spinach
¼ cup butter or margarine
3 tablespoons chopped onion
¼ cup flour
1¼ teaspoons salt
⅛ teaspoon nutmeg
⅛ teaspoon pepper
1½ cups milk
3 eggs, separated
2 tablespoons lemon juice
Hollandaise, Cheese or Egg Sauce (page 66)
   as desired

Chop spinach very fine in blender or put through food mill. Melt butter or margarine in heavy saucepan over moderate heat; add onion and cook just until tender. Stir in flour, salt, nutmeg and pepper; mix well. Add milk and cook until thick and smooth, stirring constantly. Add a small amount of sauce to beaten egg yolks; mix. Stir egg yolk mixture, spinach and lemon juice into remaining sauce. Beat egg whites until they form soft peaks. Carefully fold into spinach mixture. Pour into well-buttered 1½-quart soufflé dish or casserole. Set in pan of hot water; bake in moderate oven (375°F.) 35 to 40 minutes or until done. A knife inserted in center will come out clean when soufflé is done. Serve with Hollandaise, Cheese or Egg Sauce. Yield: 8 servings.

Carrot Soufflé

⅓ cup butter or margarine
⅓ cup flour
1 teaspoon salt
Dash of pepper
2 cups milk
½ teaspoon grated onion
4 eggs, separated
2 cups mashed cooked carrots

Melt butter or margarine in heavy saucepan over moderate heat. Stir in flour, salt and pepper. Add milk and onion. Cook until thickened, stirring constantly. Beat egg yolks; stir a small amount of sauce into beaten egg yolks, mix well and stir into sauce. Cool slightly; stir in carrots. Beat egg whites until they form soft peaks. Carefully fold sauce into egg whites. Pour into buttered 1½-quart soufflé dish or casserole. Bake in moderate oven (350°F.) 45 to 60 minutes or until high and puffy, nicely browned and done. A silver knife inserted in center of soufflé will come out clean when done. Yield: 6 servings.

Cheesy Corn Soufflé

¼ cup butter or margarine
3 tablespoons flour
½ teaspoon salt
¼ teaspoon onion salt
⅓ cup milk
1 can (1 pound) cream-style corn (about 2 cups)
½ teaspoon Worcestershire sauce
2 cups shredded Cheddar cheese (½ pound)
5 eggs, separated

Melt butter or margarine in heavy saucepan over moderate heat; stir in flour and salts. Add milk, corn and Worcestershire sauce; cook until thick, stirring constantly. Remove from heat; add cheese and stir until cheese melts. Beat egg yolks until thick and lemon colored. Add egg yolks to cheese mixture gradually, stirring constantly. Beat egg whites until they form soft peaks. Carefully fold egg whites into cheese mixture. Turn into ungreased 2-quart soufflé dish or casserole. Bake in moderate oven (350°F.) 45 to 50 minutes or until puffy, browned and firm. Serve at once. Yield: 6 servings.

Swiss-Italian Soufflé

⅓ cup butter or margarine
⅓ cup flour
¾ teaspoon salt
⅛ teaspoon pepper
¼ teaspoon oregano or ⅛ teaspoon nutmeg
1½ cups milk
6 eggs, separated
1 cup shredded Swiss cheese (¼ pound)
1 cup shredded or grated Parmesan cheese
¼ teaspoon cream of tartar

Melt butter or margarine in heavy saucepan over moderate heat. Stir in flour and seasonings. Add milk and cook over moderate heat until thickened and smooth, stirring constantly. Remove from heat. Beat egg yolks slightly; stir a small amount of sauce into egg yolks then stir eggs into remaining sauce. Add Swiss cheese; beat until melted. Stir in ¾ cup plus 2 tablespoons Parmesan cheese. Cool slightly. Beat egg whites and cream of tartar in large bowl until they hold soft peaks. Carefully fold cheese sauce into egg whites. Pour into ungreased 2-quart soufflé dish or casserole. Sprinkle remaining 2 tablespoons Parmesan cheese over top. Bake in moderate oven (350°F.) about 50 minutes or until puffed, nicely browned and fairly firm to touch. Serve at once. Yield: 8 servings.

Cheese-Sour Cream Soufflé

⅓ cup butter or margarine
¾ cup sugar
1 cup (½ pint) creamed cottage cheese
1½ tablespoons lemon juice
½ teaspoon grated lemon rind
1 teaspoon vanilla
½ teaspoon salt
4 eggs, separated
¼ cup sifted flour
1 cup (½ pint) dairy sour cream

Cream butter or margarine and ½ cup sugar until light and fluffy. Beat in cottage cheese, lemon juice, lemon rind, vanilla and salt, beating until cottage cheese is very fine. Beat egg yolks well; stir into cheese mixture. Stir in flour and sour cream. Beat egg whites until they hold soft peaks. Add remaining sugar, 2 tablespoons at a time, and continue beating until egg whites are stiff and glossy. Carefully fold egg whites into creamed mixture. Pour into ungreased 2-quart soufflé dish or casserole. Place in pan of hot water. Bake in slow oven (325°F.) 70 minutes or until puffy, browned and firm. Serve warm with a favorite fruit sauce. Yield: 8 servings.

Chicken Soufflé

¼ cup butter or margarine
1 tablespoon chopped onion
¼ cup flour
1 cup milk
1 cup finely chopped cooked chicken
¾ teaspoon salt
Dash of pepper
4 eggs, separated

Melt butter or margarine in heavy saucepan over moderate heat; add onion and cook until tender. Stir in flour; add milk gradually and cook, stirring constantly, until smooth and thickened. Stir in chicken, salt and pepper. Beat egg yolks until thick and lemon colored; stir into chicken mixture. Beat egg whites until they form soft peaks; carefully fold into chicken mixture. Pour into buttered 1½-quart soufflé dish or casserole; set in a pan of hot water. Bake in moderate oven (350°F.) 45 to 50 minutes or until puffed, nicely browned and firm. Serve plain or with favorite mushroom sauce. Yield: 6 servings.

Orange Soufflé

3 eggs
¼ cup butter or margarine
⅓ cup flour
¼ teaspoon salt
1 cup milk
⅔ cup sugar
¼ cup orange juice
1 tablespoon grated orange rind
1 teaspoon grated lemon rind
Fluffy Orange Sauce (recipe follows)

Separate eggs. Melt butter or margarine in heavy saucepan over moderate heat; stir in flour and salt. Add milk; cook over low heat, stirring constantly, until mixture is very thick. Remove from heat. Beat egg yolks; add sugar gradually and beat constantly until mixture is light and fluffy. Stir in orange juice and rinds; cool. Beat egg yolk mixture into white sauce. Beat egg whites until they hold soft peaks; carefully fold into egg yolk mixture. Pour into buttered 1½-quart soufflé dish or casserole. Place in pan of hot water. Bake in slow oven (325°F.) 1 hour or until puffed, nicely browned and firm. Serve at once with Fluffy Orange Sauce. Yield: 4 to 6 servings.

Fluffy Orange Sauce

2 eggs, separated
½ cup sugar
⅓ cup orange juice
¼ cup lemon juice
1½ teaspoons grated orange rind
½ teaspoon grated lemon rind
⅛ teaspoon salt

Beat egg yolks and sugar until light and lemon colored. Stir in fruit juices, rinds and salt. Pour into saucepan; cook over low heat, stirring constantly, until thick. Beat egg whites until they hold soft peaks; fold cooked egg yolk mixture into egg whites. Serve with Orange Soufflé. Yield: About 1½ cups.

Freeze-Ahead Orange Soufflés

See photo at right

¼ cup butter or margarine
½ cup sifted flour
¼ teaspoon salt
1 cup milk
½ cup sugar
3 eggs
⅓ cup orange juce
1 tablespoon lemon juice
4 teaspoons grated orange rind
1 teaspoon grated lemon rind
3 tablespoons orange flavored liqueur (Cointreau or Grand Marnier)

Melt butter or margarine in heavy saucepan over moderate heat. Stir in flour and salt. Add milk and ¼ cup sugar; cook, stirring constantly, until thick. Remove from heat. Separate eggs. Beat egg yolks, orange and lemon juice, rinds and liqueur; beat well. Beat hot sauce into egg yolk mixture beating constantly. Beat egg whites until they hold soft peaks. Add remaining ¼ cup sugar, a tablespoonful at a time, and beat until whites are stiff and glossy. Fold egg yolk mixture into whites. Pour into 6-ounce custard or soufflé cups. Freeze. Wrap in plastic film; seal and date. To serve, remove wrapping; set dishes in pan of hot water. Bake in moderate oven (350°F.) about 1 hour or until puffed, brown, and firm. Serve at once with the following Orange Sauce. Yield: 6 to 8 servings.

Orange Sauce

½ cup sugar
1½ tablespoons cornstarch
1 cup orange juice
½ cup water
1 tablespoon grated orange rind
¼ cup orange flavored liqueur (Cointreau or Grand Marnier), optional

Combine and mix sugar and cornstarch in saucepan. Stir in orange juice and water. Cook over low heat, stirring constantly, until thickened and clear. Stir in orange rind and liqueur, if used. Serve with Freeze-Ahead Orange Soufflés. Yield: About 1½ cups sauce.

Bacon Corn Soufflé

6 slices bacon, diced
⅓ cup finely chopped onion
¼ cup finely chopped green pepper
1 can (1 pound) cream-style corn (about 2 cups)
2 cups cooked blanched rice, drained
¾ teaspoon salt
⅛ teaspoon pepper
3 eggs, separated

Combine bacon, onion and green pepper in heavy fry pan; cook until bacon is browned and vegetables tender. Remove from heat; drain off drippings. Stir in corn, rice, salt, pepper and beaten egg yolks. Beat egg whites until they hold soft peaks. Carefully fold egg whites into corn-rice mixture. Pour into buttered 1½-quart shallow baking dish. Bake in hot oven (400°F.) 20 to 25 minutes or until crust is brown and mixture firm. Cut into squares; serve. Yield: 6 servings.

Freeze-Ahead Orange Soufflés

Fresh Rhubarb Soufflé

1 cup sugar
1 cup hot water
4 cups sliced (1-inch) fresh rhubarb
2 tablespoons cornstarch
2 tablespoons cold water
½ teaspoon vanilla
4 eggs, separated
1 cup milk, scalded
3 tablespoons lemon juice
1 teaspoon grated lemon rind
1 cup whipped cream or dessert topping, optional

Combine ½ cup sugar and hot water in heavy saucepan; bring to boil over moderate heat. Add rhubarb, simmer gently until rhubarb is almost tender. Carefully lift rhubarb pieces out of pan with slotted spoon; drain and place in 2-quart soufflé dish or casserole; save rhubarb liquid. Mix cornstarch and cold water until smooth. Stir into rhubarb liquid; cook slowly until thickened and clear, stirring constantly. Stir in vanilla; pour over rhubarb. Cool. Beat egg yolks until light and lemon colored; add remaining ½ cup sugar gradually beating during addition. Pour into a heavy saucepan. Add hot milk to egg yolks in fine stream, stirring constantly. Place over low heat; cook slowly until mixture is consistency of soft custard, stirring constantly. Cool slightly. Stir in lemon juice and rind. Beat egg whites until they hold soft peaks. Carefully fold egg whites into custard. Pour over rhubarb in soufflé dish. Bake in moderate oven (350°F.) 50 to 60 minutes or until high, lightly browned and firm. Serve at once, plain or with whipped cream or dessert topping. Yield: 6 servings.

Soufflé Grand Marnier

3 tablespoons butter or margarine
¼ cup flour
⅛ teaspoon salt
1 cup half and half (half milk, half cream)
½ cup granulated sugar
⅓ cup Grand Marnier
1 teaspoon grated orange rind
¼ teaspoon grated lemon rind
4 egg yolks
6 egg whites
Confectioners' sugar
Sweetened fresh raspberries or sliced strawberries,
    optional

Melt butter or margarine in heavy saucepan; stir in flour and salt. Add half and half and granulated sugar; cook, stirring constantly, until thick and smooth. Remove from heat; stir in Grand Marnier and fruit rinds. Beat egg yolks into mixture, one at a time, beating well after each addition. Beat egg whites until they hold soft peaks; carefully fold whites into egg yolk mixture. Turn into 2-quart soufflé dish. Sprinkle top lightly with confectioners' sugar. Place in pan of hot water. Bake in moderate oven (350°F.) 45 minutes, or until puffed, delicately browned and done. Serve at once, with fruit to spoon over soufflé, if desired. Yield: 6 to 8 servings.

Lemon Soufflé with Sauce Framboise

5 tablespoons butter or margarine
½ cup granulated sugar
¼ cup flour
¼ teaspoon salt
1 cup milk
¼ cup lemon juice
1 tablespoon grated lemon rind
4 egg yolks
7 egg whites
Confectioners' sugar
Sauce Framboise (recipe follows)

Butter inside of 2-quart soufflé dish or casserole using 1 tablespoon butter or margarine. Dust with 2 tablespoons granulated sugar. Melt remaining butter or margarine in heavy saucepan over moderate heat. Stir in flour and salt. Add milk and remaining granulated sugar; cook over low heat, stirring constantly, until mixture is thick. Remove from heat; stir in lemon juice and rind. Add egg yolks, one at a time, and beat well after each addition. Beat egg whites until they hold soft peaks. Carefully fold whites into lemon mixture. Turn into prepared dish. Place in pan of hot water; bake in moderate oven (375°F.) 40 to 45 minutes, or until browned and done. Dust top with confectioners' sugar. Serve at once with Sauce Framboise. Yield: 6 to 8 servings.

Sauce Framboise

1 egg yolk
1 egg
⅓ cup sugar
3 tablespoons Framboise or raspberry brandy

Combine ingredients in top of small double boiler; beat well. Cook over simmering water and beat constantly, until sauce holds soft peaks, 7 to 10 minutes. Serve warm. Yield: About 1 cup sauce.

Date Soufflé

¼ cup butter or margarine
⅓ cup flour
½ teaspoon salt
1 cup milk
3 eggs, separated
1½ tablespoons lemon juice
½ cup thinly sliced pitted dates
½ cup sugar
1 cup sweetened whipped cream, optional

Melt butter or margarine in saucepan; stir in flour, salt and milk; cook over low heat until thickened and smooth, stirring constantly. Cool. Add beaten egg yolks, lemon juice and dates. Beat egg whites until they hold stiff peaks. Add sugar, 2 tablespoons at a time, beating well after each addition. Fold into egg yolk mixture. Pour into well-greased 2-quart soufflé dish or casserole. Place in a pan of hot water. Bake in slow oven (325°F.) 1 hour or until puffed, browned and fairly firm. Serve at once, plain or with whipped cream. Yield: 6-8 servings.

Chocolate Soufflé

⅓ cup butter or margarine
1 cup plus 2 tablespoons sugar
⅓ cup flour
½ cup cocoa
1½ cups milk
6 eggs, separated
2 teaspoons vanilla
¼ teaspoon cream of tartar
¼ teaspoon salt
½ cup finely chopped pecans or walnuts
1 cup sweetened whipped cream

Butter bottom and sides of 2-quart soufflé dish using 1 tablespoon butter or margarine; sprinkle evenly with 2 tablespoons sugar. Melt remaining butter or margarine in heavy saucepan; remove from heat. Stir flour and cocoa into melted butter or margarine. Add milk gradually and cook over low heat until thickened and smooth, stirring constantly. Remove from heat; cool about 10 minutes, stirring frequently. Whip egg yolks, ½ cup sugar and vanilla until thick and lemon colored. Beat in cocoa mixture. Beat egg whites, cream of tartar and salt until they hold soft peaks. Add remaining ½ cup sugar gradually beating constantly until stiff and glossy. Carefully fold cocoa mixture and nuts into egg whites. Pour into soufflé dish. Place in pan of hot water. Bake in moderate oven (350°F.) about 1¼ hours or until knife inserted in center comes out clean. Serve at once with whipped cream. Yield: 8 to 10 servings.

Orange Sweet Potato Soufflé

½ cup milk
3 tablespoons butter or margarine
4 cups mashed canned or fresh cooked sweet potatoes
4 eggs, separated
⅔ cup sugar
⅓ cup sherry
4 teaspoons grated orange rind
1 teaspoon salt
1 teaspoon vanilla
1 cup finely chopped pecans or walnuts
Whipped cream or dessert topping, optional

Combine milk and butter or margarine in saucepan. Place over low heat until butter or margarine melts. Beat into sweet potatoes. Combine egg yolks, sugar, sherry, orange rind, salt and vanilla; beat lightly. Whip into sweet potatoes. Stir in nuts. Beat egg whites until they hold soft peaks; carefully fold into sweet potato mixture. Pour into 2-quart soufflé or casserole dish. Bake in hot oven (400°F.) 50 minutes or until done. Soufflé is done when knife inserted in center of the dish comes out clean. Serve at once, plain or with whipped cream or dessert topping. Yield: 8 servings.

BRANDIED SWEET POTATO SOUFFLÉ: Follow recipe for Orange Sweet Potato Soufflé and substitute 2 teaspoons grated lemon for orange rind and brandy for sherry.

Apple Soufflé with Fresh Fruit Sauce

2 envelopes (2 tablespoons) unflavored gelatin
2½ cups apple juice
8 eggs, separated
1¼ cups sugar
1¼ teaspoons salt
1¼ teaspoons vanilla
2 cups whipped cream or dessert topping
1½ cups sugared fresh raspberries, sliced peaches
  or strawberries

Tape or tie a 3-inch waxed paper band snugly around outside edge of 1½-quart soufflé dish or casserole. Soak gelatin in ½ cup cold apple juice 5 minutes; mix. Beat egg yolks and ½ cup sugar slightly; pour into heavy saucepan. Stir in 2 cups cold apple juice. Place over low heat; cook, stirring constantly until mixture coats spoon. Add gelatin; stir until dissolved. Cool until it becomes syrupy and starts to set around edge of pan. Beat egg whites and salt until they form soft peaks. Add remaining ¾ sugar gradually beating constantly until mixture is stiff and glossy. Stir vanilla into egg yolk mixture; beat until fluffy. Fold egg whites and whipped cream or dessert topping into egg yolk mixture. Turn into prepared dish. Chill until firm. Carefully remove waxed paper collar. Garnish and serve with fruit. Yield: 8 to 10 servings.

Coffee Nut Soufflés

2 envelopes (2 tablespoons) unflavored gelatin
3 cups milk
1⅓ cups sugar
¼ cup instant coffee powder
¼ teaspoon salt
4 eggs, separated
2½ teaspoons vanilla
2 cups whipping cream
½ cup finely chopped toasted almonds or pecans
Chocolate curls

Tape or tie a 3-inch wide double thick waxed paper band around top of twelve 4-ounce or eight 6-ounce soufflé or dessert dishes allowing collar to stand 1 inch above edge of dish. Sprinkle gelatin over ½ cup cold milk; stir and let stand 5 minutes. Combine 1 cup sugar, coffee powder and salt in heavy saucepan. Beat egg yolks slightly; stir in remaining milk and add to sugar-coffee mixture. Cook over low heat until mixture thickens slightly, stirring constantly. Add gelatin and stir until it dissolves. Remove from heat; stir in vanilla. Chill until syrupy stirring often. Beat egg whites until they hold soft peaks. Add remaining ⅓ cup sugar to egg whites, a tablespoon at a time; beat well after each addition. Fold into coffee mixture. Whip cream until stiff; fold in nuts and fold into coffee mixture. Spoon into prepared dishes to top of collar. Chill until set. Before serving remove collars from desserts carefully and garnish top with chocolate curls. Yield: 8 to 12 servings.

Chilled Orange Soufflés

1 can (1 pound) apricot halves
Orange juice
4 eggs, separated
¾ cup sugar
½ teaspoon salt
2 envelopes (1 tablespoon each) unflavored gelatin
1 tablespoon grated orange rind
1 cup whipping cream, whipped
Small orange sections, optional
Mint sprigs, optional

Tie or tape double thick collar of waxed paper 2-inches wide tightly around edge of 8 small individual soufflé dishes, coffee or custard cups; fasten securely. Drain apricots; save syrup. Add orange juice as needed to make 1 cup liquid. Beat egg yolks, ½ cup sugar and salt; beat slightly, pour into saucepan. Stir in liquids and gelatin. Cook over low heat until mixture coats a spoon, stirring constantly. Mash apricots. Stir into cooked mixture. Add orange rind. Chill until mixture starts to thicken. Beat egg whites until they hold soft peaks. Add remaining ¼ cup sugar, a small amount at a time, and continue beating until egg whites are stiff and glossy. Fold gelatin mixture and whipped cream into egg whites. Spoon into dishes. Chill until firm. Remove waxed paper collars carefully. Garnish with small orange sections and mint sprigs, if desired. Yield: 8 servings.

Strawberry Soufflé

1 package (10 ounce) frozen strawberry halves, defrosted
Water
1 envelope (1 tablespoon) unflavored gelatin
4 eggs, separated
¾ cup sugar
¼ teaspoon salt
2 teaspoons lemon juice
¾ teaspoon vanilla
Red food color, as desired
1 cup (½ pint) whipping cream, whipped
Thawed sweetened strawberries or sweetened whipped cream, as desired

Drain strawberries; reserve liquid. Add water as needed to strawberry juice to make ¾ cup liquid; pour into saucepan. Mash strawberries. Sprinkle gelatin over strawberry liquid in saucepan. Combine egg yolks, ¼ cup sugar and salt; beat slightly. Stir into gelatin mixture; mix well. Cook over low heat, stirring constantly until mixture is slightly thickened. Remove from heat; stir in strawberries, lemon juice and vanilla. Tint an attractive pink with red food color. Chill until mixture begins to set. Beat egg whites until they hold soft peaks. Add remaining ½ cup sugar gradually, beating constantly until egg whites are stiff and glossy. Carefully fold into gelatin mixture. Fold in whipped cream. Turn into 1½-quart soufflé dish. Chill until firm. Serve plain or topped with defrosted frozen sweetened strawberries or sweetened whipped cream, as desired. Yield: 8 to 10 servings.

RASPBERRY SOUFFLÉ: Follow recipe for Strawberry Soufflé (this page). Substitute 1 package (10 ounce) frozen red raspberries, defrosted, for strawberries. Serve with additional defrosted frozen red raspberries, if desired.

Lemon or Lime Soufflés

½ cup cold water
1 envelope (1 tablespoon) unflavored gelatin
¾ cup sugar
½ teaspoon salt
4 eggs, separated
1 can (6 ounce) defrosted frozen lemonade or limeade concentrate
1 cup (½ pint) whipping cream, whipped
Toasted flaked or shredded coconut

Tape or tie a collar of double thick waxed paper around top of six 5-ounce individual soufflé or dessert dishes so it will extend 1 inch above edge of dish. Pour water into saucepan. Sprinkle gelatin over water. Combine ½ cup sugar, salt and egg yolks; beat slightly. Stir into gelatin; mix well. Cook over low heat, stirring constantly until mixture coats spoon. Stir in undiluted lemonade or limeade. Chill until mixture begins to set. Beat egg whites until they form soft peaks. Add remaining ¼ cup sugar gradually, beating constantly until egg whites are stiff and glossy. Carefully fold into gelatin mixture. Fold in whipped cream. Spoon into prepared dishes. Sprinkle with coconut. Chill until set. Carefully remove collars from desserts. Yield: 6 servings.

Chocolate Crème de Menthe Soufflé

1 envelope (1 tablespoon) unflavored gelatin
1⅓ cups sugar
½ teaspoon salt
1 cup milk
5 eggs, separated
1 bar (4 ounce) German's sweet chocolate, melted and cooled
¼ cup Crème de Menthe or ½ teaspoon peppermint extract
1 teaspoon vanilla
1 cup (½ pint) whipping cream, whipped
1 cup sweetened whipped cream, for garnish, if desired

Combine gelatin, 1 cup sugar and salt in saucepan; mix. Stir in milk and slightly beaten egg yolks. Cook over low heat, stirring constantly, until mixture is thickened and coats a spoon. Remove from heat. Stir in chocolate and flavorings. Chill until mixture begins to set. Beat egg whites until they hold soft peaks. Add remaining ⅓ cup sugar gradually, beating constantly until egg whites are stiff and glossy. Carefully fold into chocolate mixture. Fold in whipped cream. Turn into 1½-quart soufflé dish. Chill until firm. Serve plain or topped with sweetened whipped cream, as desired. Yield: 8 to 10 servings.

CHOCOLATE RUM SOUFFLÉ: Follow recipe for Chocolate Crème de Menthe Soufflé. Substitute ¼ cup rum or ½ teaspoon rum extract for Crème de Menthe or peppermint extract.

Egg Noodles

2 cups sifted flour
1 teaspoon salt
3 medium eggs
3 tablespoons water

Sift together flour and salt. Combine eggs and water; beat well. Add flour mixture to make very stiff dough. Knead on lightly floured board about 1 minute or until elastic. Let rest 10 minutes. Roll out as thin as possible. Let stand about 1 hour or until partially dry, turning once. Follow directions with noodle maker or roll up dough and slice in desired width, ⅛ to ½ inch. Toss noodles lightly to separate strips and allow to dry. Yield: About 5 cups.

INDEX